ORIGAMI
AND MATH
SIMPLE TO COMPLEX

ORIGAMI
AND MATH
SIMPLE TO COMPLEX

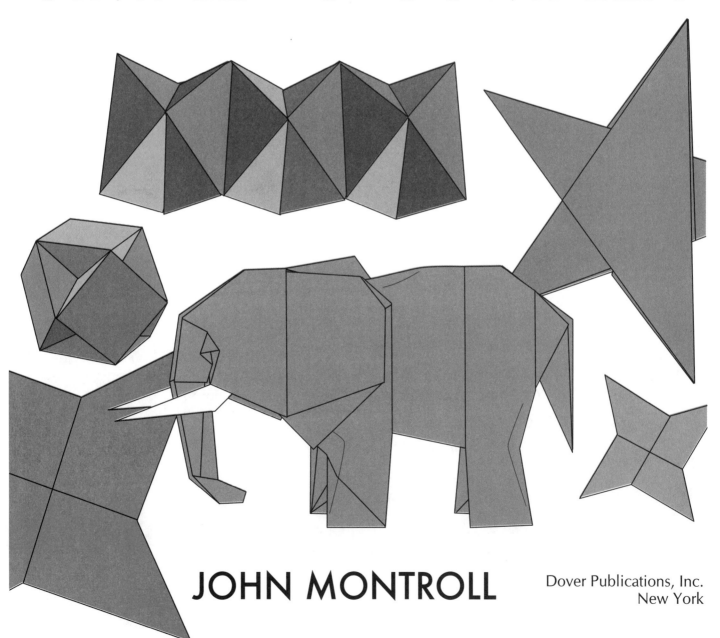

JOHN MONTROLL

Dover Publications, Inc.
New York

To Charley and Kimmy

Bibliographical Note

Origami and Math is a new work, first published in
separate editions by Antroll Publishing Company,
Maryland, and Dover Publications, Inc.,New York in 2012.

International Standard Book Number

ISBN-13: 978-0-486-48886-8
ISBN-10: 0-486-48886-1

Manufactured in the United States of America
www.doverpublications.com

Introduction

ath, art, and nature combine to create the unimaginable. Huge galaxies spin, birds fly, eagles have keen vision, and amoeba divide. But we do origami. By adding math to origami, it can be further developed for elegance, design, and new possibilities. This book explores these possibilities.

In the first part of the book we investigate geometric models. There are polygons including the cubehemioctahedron. There are methods to divide the square into nths. There are chess boards, ranging from a silly 1 × 1 to a playable 8 × 8. There is an investigation into five-sided origami, including a variety of stars and flowers. Thus math is very useful for figuring out how to fold these geometric models.

In the second part, math is used for designing origami animals. We will show mathematical techniques for adapting origami structures to correct animal proportions. Using this, we are able to create an elephant with the correct proportions. These techniques also help us depict the differences between a one and two humped camel. So seemingly trivial changes at the start have far-reaching implications for the final model.

Each model is folded from a square, leading to the math involved. Also described is my method for On the Edge, a procedure for finding the most efficient folding method to locate any point on the edge of a square sheet.

The diagrams conform to the internationally approved Randlett-Yoshizawa style. Although any square paper can be used for the projects in this book, the best material is origami paper. Origami supplies can be found in arts and craft shops, or visit Dover Publications online at www.doverpublications.com, or OrigamiUSA at www.origami-usa.org.

Many people helped make this book possible. I thank Bob Vaughn for his creative input and also my editor, Jan Polish. Of course I also thank the many folders who proofread the diagrams.

I hope you will enjoy folding and making new discoveries.

John Montroll

www.johnmontroll.com

Contents

Polygons *page 10*

**Equilateral
Triangle**
★
page 11

Pentagon
★
page 12

Hexagon
★
page 13

Heptagon
★
page 14

Octagon
★
page 15

Decagon
★
page 16

Dodecagon
★
page 17

**Silver
Rhombus**
★
page 18

**Silver
Rectangle**
★
page 18

**Bronze
Rectangle**
★
page 19

**Golden
Rectangle**
★
page 19

Dividing the Square into *n*ths *page 20*

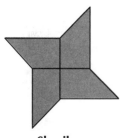

Shuriken
★★
page 23

Cubehemioctahedron
★★
page 25

Cubicles
★★★★
page 27

**Triangular
Troublewit**
★★
page 31

**Square
Troublewit**
★★
page 32

**Pentagonal
Troublewit**
★★
page 37

Chess Boards *page 40*

1 × 1 Chess Board
page 41

2 × 2 Chess Board
★★
page 41

3 × 3 Chess Board
★★
page 43

4 × 4 Chess Board
★★★
page 46

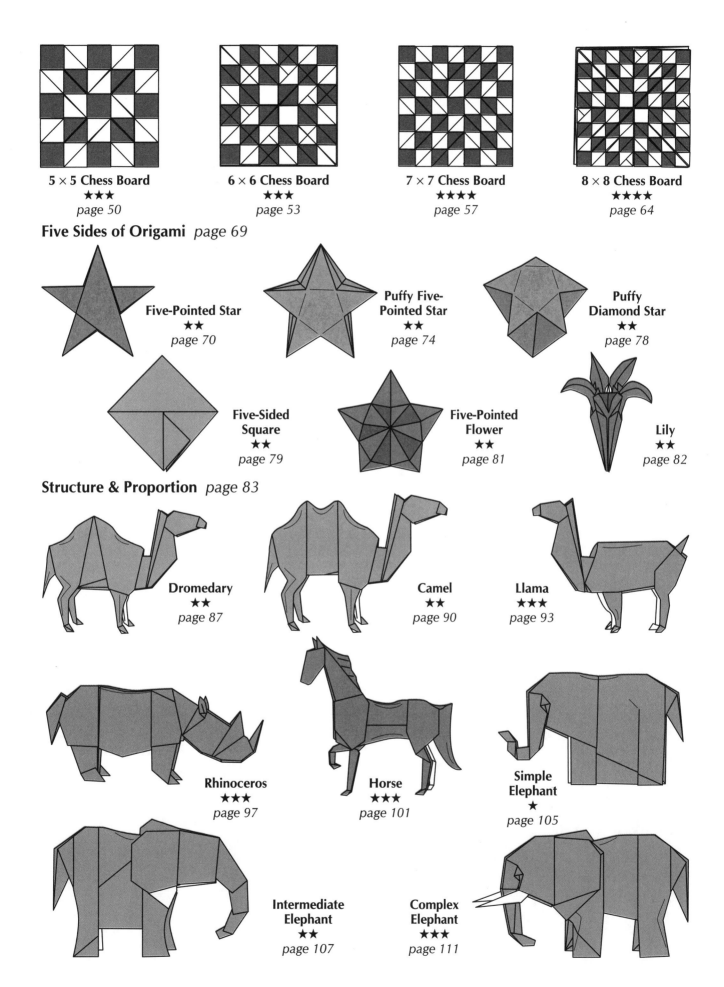

Contents   7

Symbols

Lines

– – – – – – – – – –   Valley fold, fold in front.

– · – · · – · – · · –   Mountain fold, fold behind.

─────────────   Crease line.

····························   X-ray or guide line.

Arrows

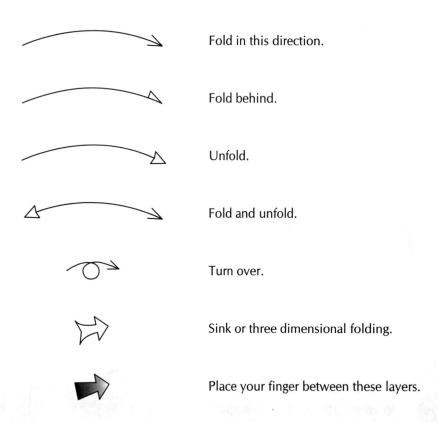

Fold in this direction.

Fold behind.

Unfold.

Fold and unfold.

Turn over.

Sink or three dimensional folding.

Place your finger between these layers.

Origami & Math

Origami lends itself to math. Starting with a square, a simple geometric shape, each fold can be represented mathematically, as can the overall design. We will explore several topics, dealing with angles, dividing into *n*ths, finding landmarks, and concepts of structure and proportion for animals.

To use math on the square paper, consider the square to be of size 1 × 1. Here are some simple angles and landmarks.

45° and 22.5°, used for animals.

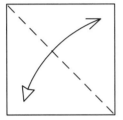

1   Fold and unfold.

2   Fold to the crease.

3   Unfold.

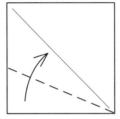

4   22.5° and 45°

$$\tan(22.5°) = \sqrt{2} - 1 \approx .41421$$

Length of each side is 1.

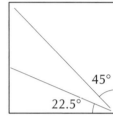

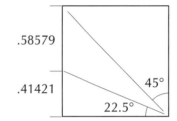

15° and 30°, used for geometrics.

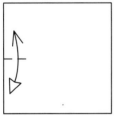

1   Fold and unfold on the left.

2   Bring the corners to the crease.

3   Unfold.

4   15° and 30°

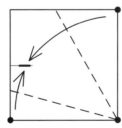

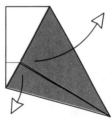

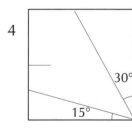

$$\tan(30°) = 1/\sqrt{3} \approx .57735$$

$$\tan(15°) = 2 - \sqrt{3} \approx .26795$$

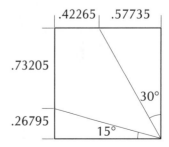

Polygons

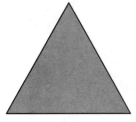
Equilateral Triangle

Pentagon

Decagon

Silver Rhombus

Polygons are beautiful shapes in themselves and can be used as bases for more models.
I will present several uniform polygons along with a rhombus and three rectangles.

Designing polygons requires some math. A uniform polygon can be divided into triangles radiating from a vertex so that all the angles, α, at that vertex are congruent.

If an odd-sided polygon is inscribed in a square so the vertex is top center, then two other vertices meet the edges. The angles at the top outside the polygon are also the same. This is the key to creating them.

For example, consider the heptagon.

The heptagon is divided into five triangles, all with equal angles at the vertex.

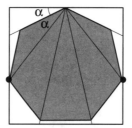

From the top center of the square, the paper is divided into seven equal angles to generate the heptagon. Two vertices meet the edge of the square on the left and right.

Polygons can be used as models on their own, as coasters to place standing models, or as bases to create more. I encourage you to make new figures such as ornaments or flowers. There are many ideas that can apply to several polygons so you can make similar flowers, stars, bowls, etc, with different number of points.

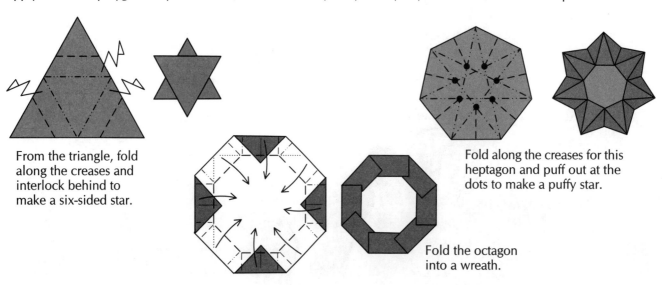

From the triangle, fold along the creases and interlock behind to make a six-sided star.

Fold the octagon into a wreath.

Fold along the creases for this heptagon and puff out at the dots to make a puffy star.

Equilateral Triangle

# of sides: 3
Angle at vertex: 60°

Here are two equilateral triangles folded from a square. The first uses book-fold symmetry, the second uses diagonal symmetry resulting in a slightly larger triangle.

Book-fold symmetry

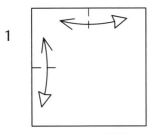

1 Fold and unfold in half on two edges.

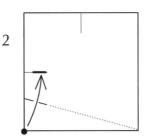

2 Bring the dot to the crease. Crease on the left.

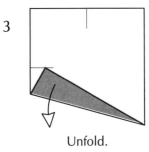

3 Unfold.

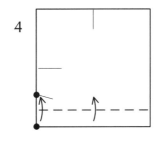

4

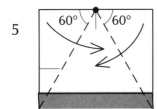

5

6

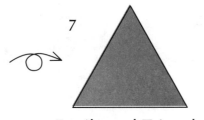

7

Equilateral Triangle

Diagonal symmetry

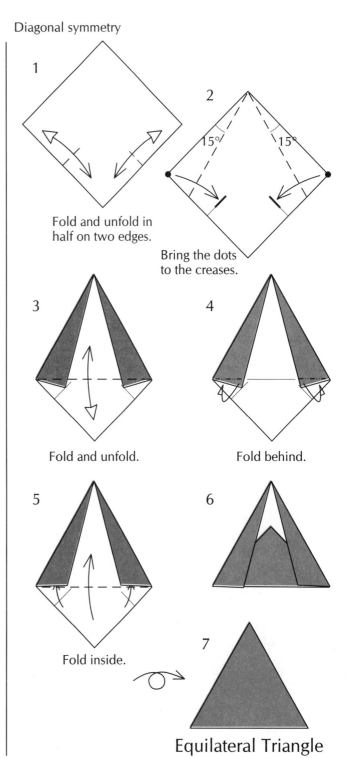

1 Fold and unfold in half on two edges.

2 Bring the dots to the creases.

3 Fold and unfold.

4 Fold behind.

5 Fold inside.

6

7

Equilateral Triangle

Pentagon

# of sides: 5
Angle at vertex: 108°
Angle α: 36°

This method for folding a pentagon is exact, with only a few folds. My procedure, On the Edge (page 116), was used to find an efficient folding sequence to locate landmark a.

$$a = 1 - .5 \tan(36°)$$
$$\approx .36327$$

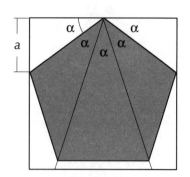

1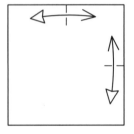

Fold and unfold on two edges.

2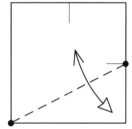

Fold and unfold, creasing lightly.

3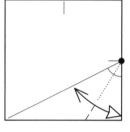

Fold and unfold at the bottom to bisect the angle.

4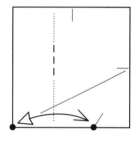

Fold and unfold in the center.

5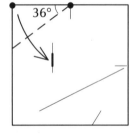

Bring the corner to the crease. The 36° angle is exact.

6

Fold and unfold.

7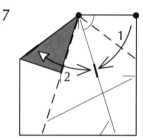

1. Fold to the crease.
2. Fold and unfold.

8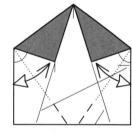

Fold and unfold at the bottom to bisect the angles.

9

Bisect the angles.

10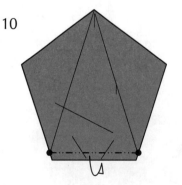

11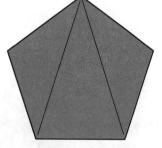

Pentagon

Hexagon

# of sides: 6
Angle at vertex: 120°

Here are two hexagons folded from a square. The first uses book-fold symmetry, the second uses diagonal symmetry resulting in a slightly larger hexagon.

Book-fold symmetry

1

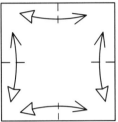

Fold and unfold in half on the edges.

2

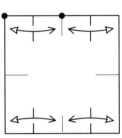

Fold and unfold.

3

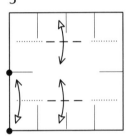

Fold and unfold in the center.

4

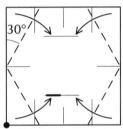

30°

Fold the corners to the creases.

5

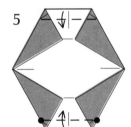

6

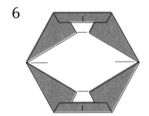

7

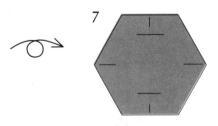

Hexagon

Diagonal symmetry

1

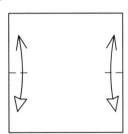

Fold and unfold on the edges.

2

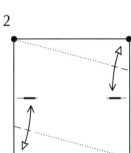

Bring the corners to the creases. Fold and unfold on the edges.

3

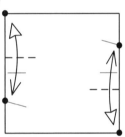

Fold and unfold on the left and right.

4

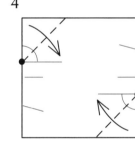

5

Fold and unfold on the edges.

6

15°

7

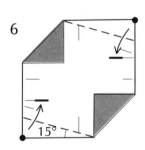

8

Hexagon

Heptagon

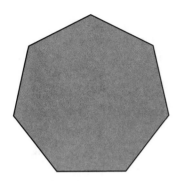

# of sides: 7
Angle at vertex: 128.57°
Angle α: 180°/7 ≈ 25.71°

Length a is calculated and a folding sequence is found from my routine, On the Edge (page 116). This landmark is the key to folding the heptagon.

$$a = 1 - .5 \tan(360°/7)$$
$$\approx .37302$$

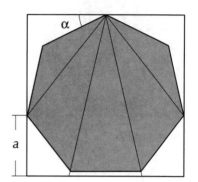

1

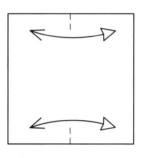

Fold and unfold on the edges.

2

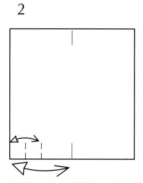

Fold and unfold in half twice, on the bottom.

3

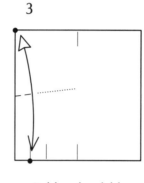

Fold and unfold on the left.

4

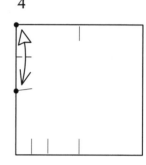

Fold and unfold on the left.

5

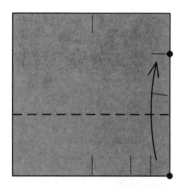

6

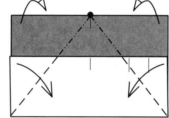

7

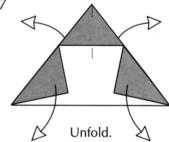

Unfold.

8

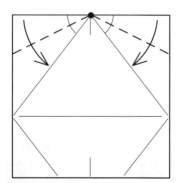

9

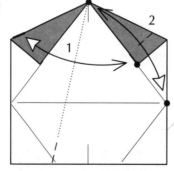

Fold and unfold at the bottom and on the right.

10

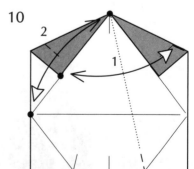

Fold and unfold at the bottom and on the left.

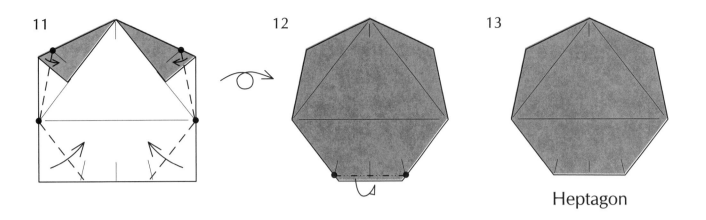

11

12

13

Heptagon

Octagon

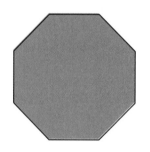

# of sides: 8
Angle at vertex: 135°

The folding is simple and exact.

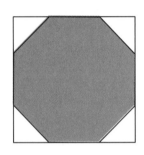

1

Fold and unfold
by the corners.

2

Crease on the left.

3

4

Unfold and rotate 90°.

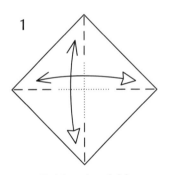

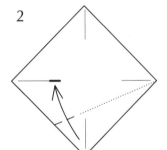

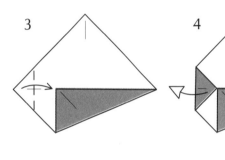

5

Repeat steps 2–4
three more times.

6

Refold.

7

8

Octagon

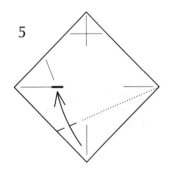

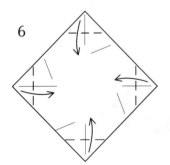

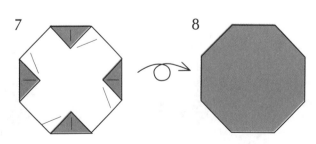

Decagon

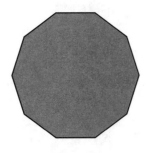

# of sides: 10
Angle at vertex: 144°
Angle α: 18°

This method for folding
a decagon is exact.

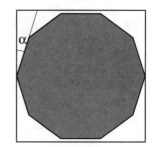

1
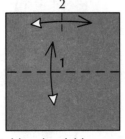

1. Fold and unfold.
2. Fold and unfold at the top.

2
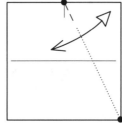

Fold and unfold
on the top.

3
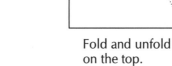

Fold and unfold on the
left to bisect the angle.

4
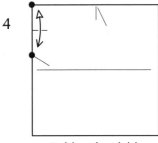

Fold and unfold
on the left.

5

1. Fold and unfold.
2. Fold behind along the crease.

6
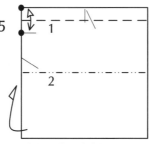

18°   18°

Bring the corners to the
crease and repeat behind.
The 18° angles are exact.

7
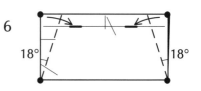

Unfold.

8

9
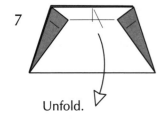 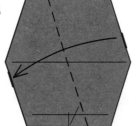

Fold along hidden edges.

10

Unfold.

11
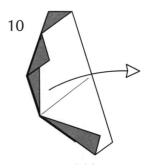

Repeat steps 8–10 in
the other direction.

12
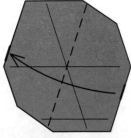

13
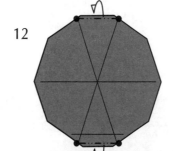 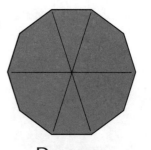

Decagon

Dodecagon

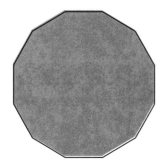

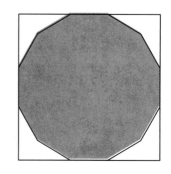

# of sides: 12
Angle at vertex: 150°

The folding is simple and exact.

1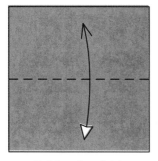

Fold and unfold.

2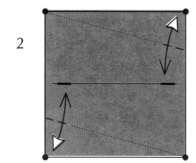

Bring the corners to the creases. Fold and unfold on the edges.

3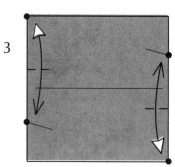

Fold and unfold on the left and right.

4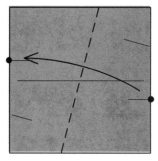

Rotate.

5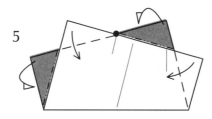

Fold along hidden edges.

6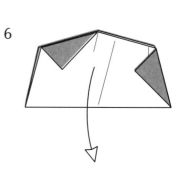

Unfold and rotate.

7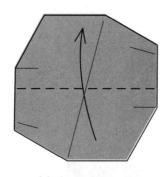

Fold along the crease.

8

Fold along hidden edges.

9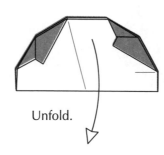

Unfold.

10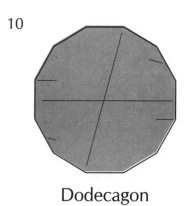

Dodecagon

Silver Rhombus

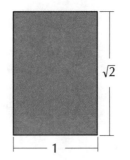

The proportions of the diagonals of the Silver Rhombus are 1 to √2.

1

Fold and unfold by the corners.

2

Crease on the left.

3

4

Unfold and rotate 180°.

5

Repeat steps 2–4.

6

Fold through the intersections.

7

8

Silver Rhombus

Silver Rectangle

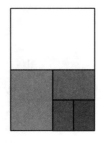

The silver rectangle has sides proportional to 1 × √2. When divided in half, each part is also a silver rectangle.

Each rectangle is a silver rectangle.

1

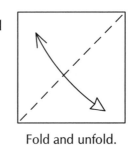

Fold and unfold.

2

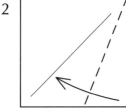

3

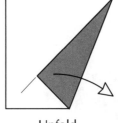

Unfold.

4

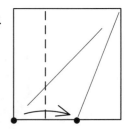

5

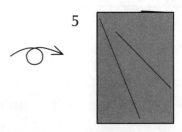

Silver Rectangle

Bronze Rectangle

Golden Rectangle

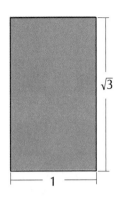

The bronze rectangle has sides proportional to $1 \times \sqrt{3}$.

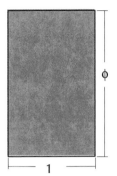

The golden rectangle has sides proportional to 1×1.618034. This is the same as $.618034 \times 1$.

The name comes from the golden mean (phi = ϕ) where

$$\phi = \frac{\sqrt{5}+1}{2} = 1.618034$$

It is the solution to

$$x - 1 = 1/x$$
$$\phi - 1 \approx .618034$$

This number is associated with nature and beauty.

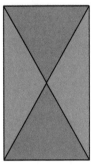

The diagonals highlight two equilateral triangles.

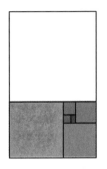

The golden rectangle divides into a square and a smaller golden rectangle.

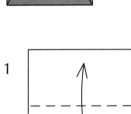

1

Fold and unfold.

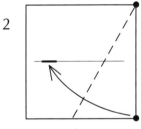

2

Bring the corner to the crease.

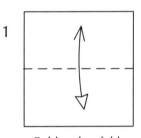

1

Fold and unfold.

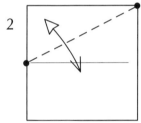

2

Fold and unfold.

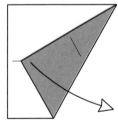

3

Unfold.

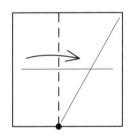

4

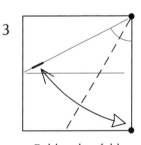

3

Fold and unfold.

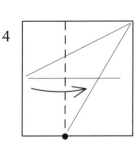

4

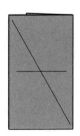

5

Bronze Rectangle

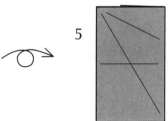

5

Golden Rectangle

Dividing the Square into *n*ths

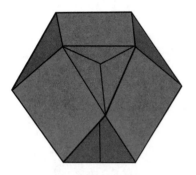

Cubehemioctahedron
Divisions of 1/5

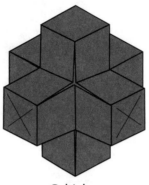

Cubicles
Divisions of 1/7

5 × 5 Chess Board
Divisions of 1/13

Many origami models are structured by dividing the paper into *n*ths, such as thirds or fifths. This includes geometrics, polyhedra, the chess boards, along with many animals. Dividing the paper in half several times is easy, but it would be good to know efficient methods for any *n*.

There are some general methods and special cases. I will begin with the diagonal method (a general method), some examples of the diagonal method, and then show some special cases.

Diagonal Method for Dividing the Square into *n*ths

To divide into *n*ths, find two numbers *a* and *b* so that
$$a + b = n$$
$$a > b.$$
In general, let $a = 2, 4, 8, \ldots$ or a power of 2.

Find length b/a
on the left edge.

1

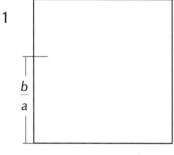

Choose *a* and *b* so
$$a + b = n$$
$$a > b$$

This method works well as
long as b/a is not too small.

Make a crease from the left edge
at b/a to the bottom right corner.

2

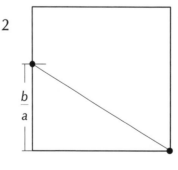

Fold and unfold along
the upper diagonal.

3

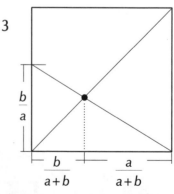

The intersection divides the
bottom into $b/(a+b)$ and $a/(a+b)$.

Examples of the Diagonal Method for Dividing the Square into *n*ths

Divisions of 1/3

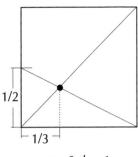

1/2

1/3

$a = 2, b = 1$

Divisions of 1/5
(see special cases)

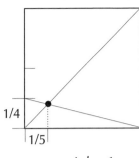

1/4

1/5

$a = 4, b = 1$

Divisions of 1/7

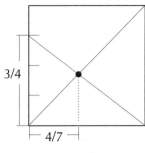

3/4

4/7

$a = 4, b = 3$

Divisions of 1/9
(see special cases)

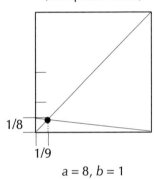

1/8

1/9

$a = 8, b = 1$

Divisions of 1/11

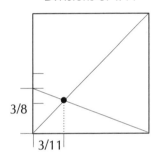

3/8

3/11

$a = 8, b = 3$

Divisions of 1/13

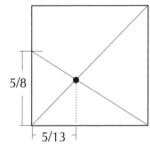

5/8

5/13

$a = 8, b = 5$

Divisions of 1/15

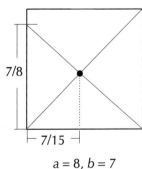

7/8

7/15

$a = 8, b = 7$

Divisions of 1/17

Here is an example where the angle is too small if *a* is a power of 2. Another choice for *a* gives good results.

If $a = 16, b = 1$, then we see this diagram. But the angle is too small to work, so we choose another pair for *a* and *b* which also add up to 17.

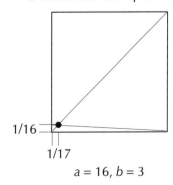

1/16

1/17

$a = 16, b = 3$

Let $a = 9, b = 8$. We can divide into 17ths much better. But first we divide in 9th which is shown in the special cases.

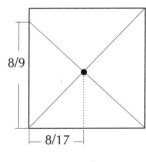

8/9

8/17

$a = 9, b = 8$

Special Cases for Dividing the Square into *n*ths

Divisions of 1/5

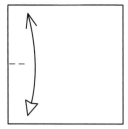

1 Fold and unfold on the left.

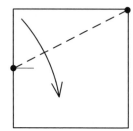

2

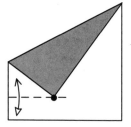

3 Fold and unfold on the right.

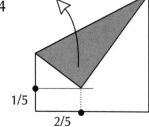

4 1/5
2/5

Unfold. The 1/5 and 2/5 marks are found.

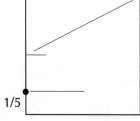

5 1/5

Divisions of 1/5.

Divisions of 1/8

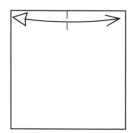

1 Fold and unfold at the top.

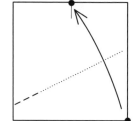

2 Fold on the left.

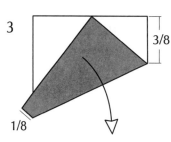

3 3/8
1/8

Unfold. The 1/8 and 3/8 marks are found.

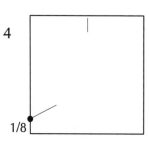

4 1/8

Divisions of 1/8.

Divisions of 1/9

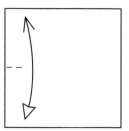

1 Fold and unfold on the left.

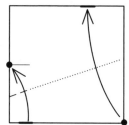

2 Bring the lower right corner to the top edge and the bottom edge to the left center. Crease on the left.

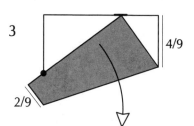

3 4/9
2/9

Unfold. The 2/9 and 4/9 marks are found.

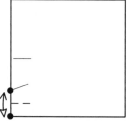

4 Fold and unfold.

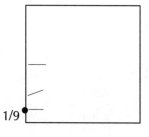

5 1/9

Divisions of 1/9.

Shuriken

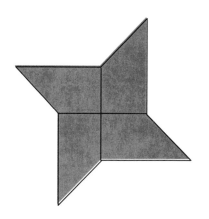

This original model is based on the traditional shuriken, which is a model of a Japanese throwing weapon. The traditional version is folded from two 1 × 4 strips which are interlocked. This one is from a single square. The paper is divided into thirds.

This design uses square symmetry. The folds and crease pattern are the same when rotated 90°.

1

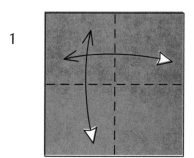

Fold and unfold.

2

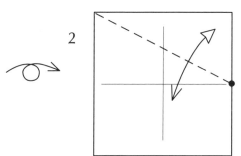

Fold and unfold.

3

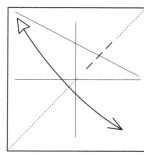

Fold and unfold creasing in the upper middle part.

4

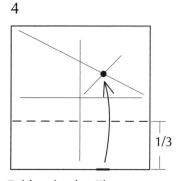

1/3

Fold to the dot. The paper is divided into thirds.

5

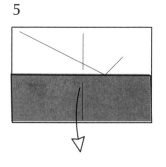

Unfold.

6

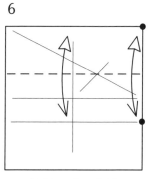

Fold and unfold. Rotate 90°.

7

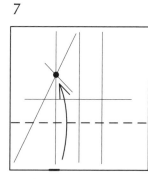

Repeat steps 4–6.

8

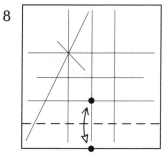

Fold and unfold.

9

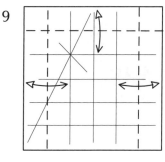

Fold and unfold. Rotate.

10

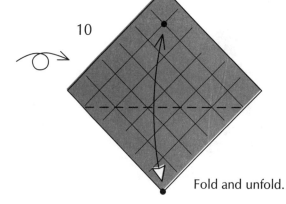

Fold and unfold.

11

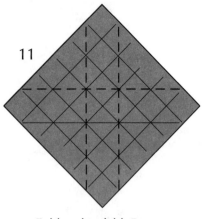

Fold and unfold. Rotate.

12

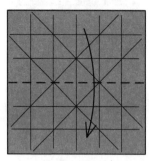

Fold in half.

13

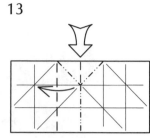

Push in at the top.

14

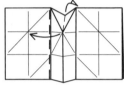

This is a 3D intermediate step.

15

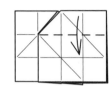

16

Fold up from behind.

17

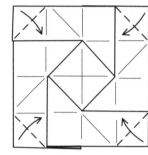

Fold the corners.

18

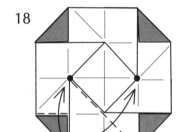

The pairs of dots will meet. Rotate 90°.

19

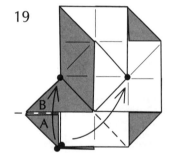

Region A will cover B. Rotate 90°.

20

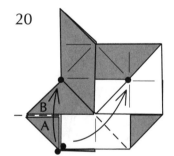

Region A will cover B. Rotate 90°.

21

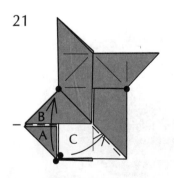

Tuck C inside.

22

23

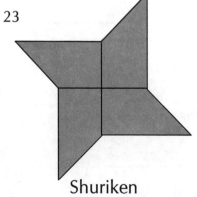

Shuriken

Cubehemioctahedron

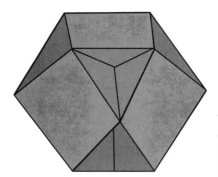

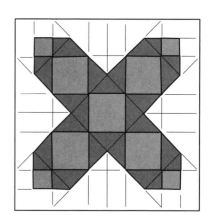

The cubehemioctahedron is basically a cube with sunken corners. This model uses square symmetry. The darker paper in the crease pattern shows the sunken sides. The paper is divided into fifths.

1

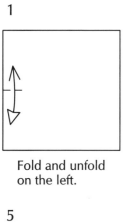

Fold and unfold on the left.

2

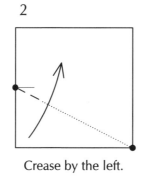

Crease by the left.

3

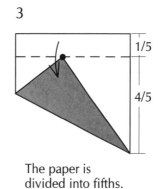

1/5
4/5

The paper is divided into fifths.

4

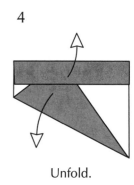

Unfold.

5

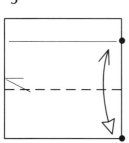

Fold and unfold.

6

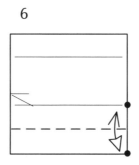

Fold and unfold.

7

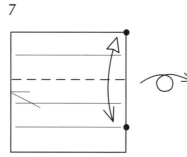

Fold and unfold.

8

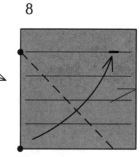

9

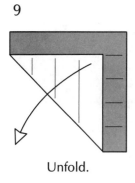

Unfold.

10

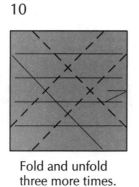

Fold and unfold three more times.

11

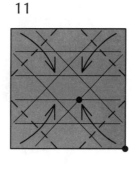

12

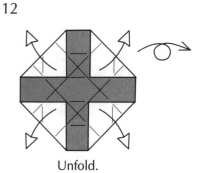

Unfold.

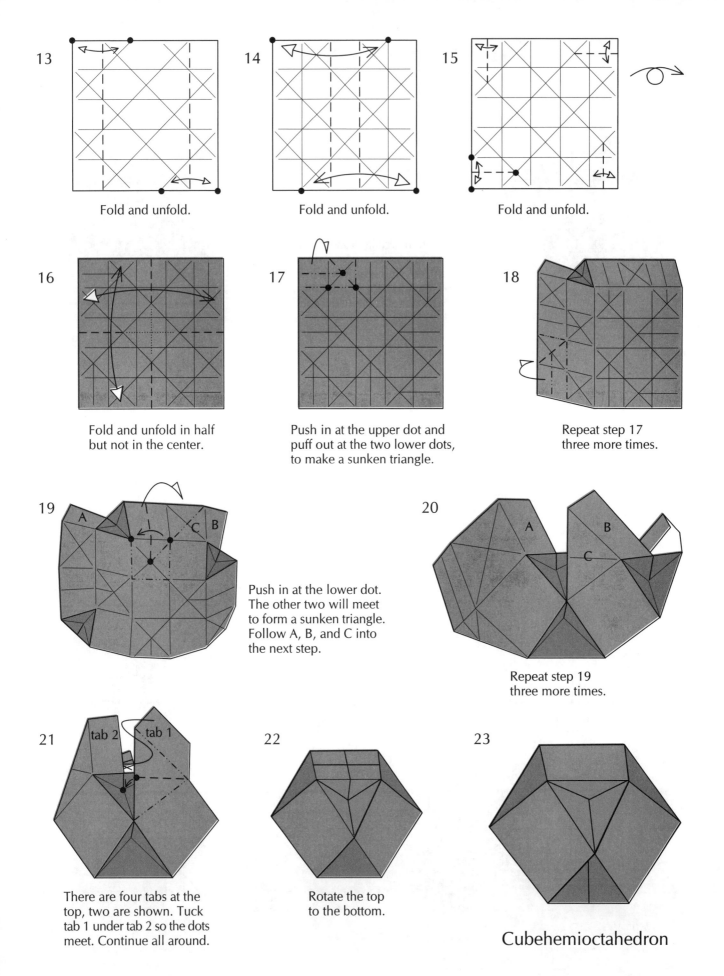

13 Fold and unfold.

14 Fold and unfold.

15 Fold and unfold.

16 Fold and unfold in half but not in the center.

17 Push in at the upper dot and puff out at the two lower dots, to make a sunken triangle.

18 Repeat step 17 three more times.

19 Push in at the lower dot. The other two will meet to form a sunken triangle. Follow A, B, and C into the next step.

20 Repeat step 19 three more times.

21 There are four tabs at the top, two are shown. Tuck tab 1 under tab 2 so the dots meet. Continue all around.

22 Rotate the top to the bottom.

23 Cubehemioctahedron

Cubicles

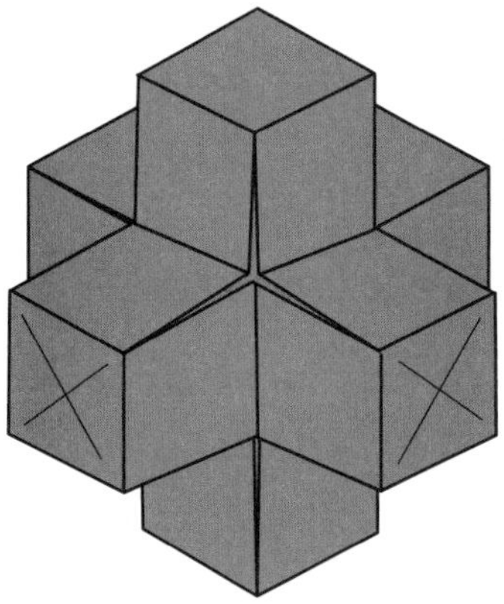

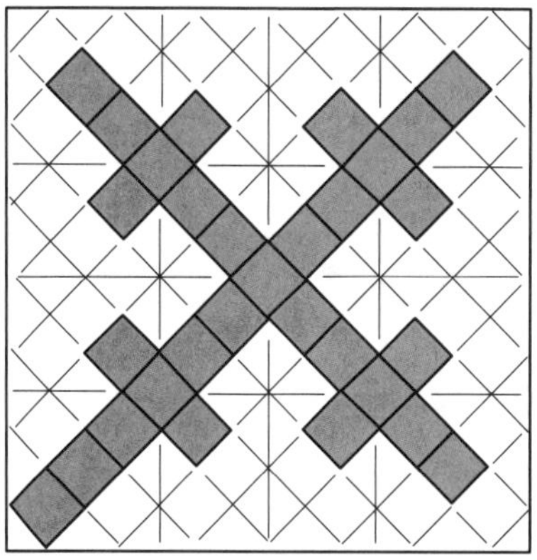

This shape is made of six cubes on the faces of a central seventh cube. This challenging model uses divisions of 1/7.

1

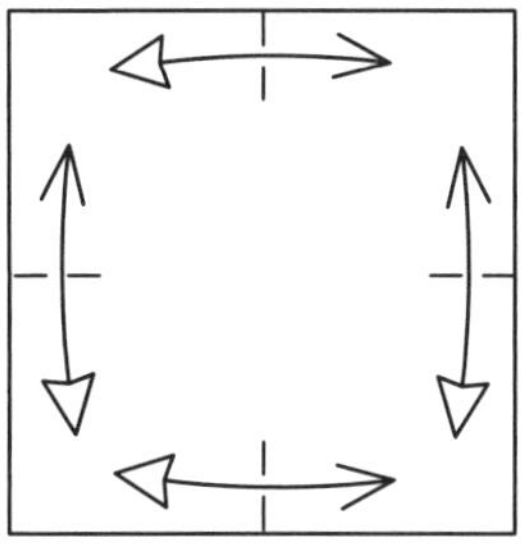

Fold and unfold on the edges.

2

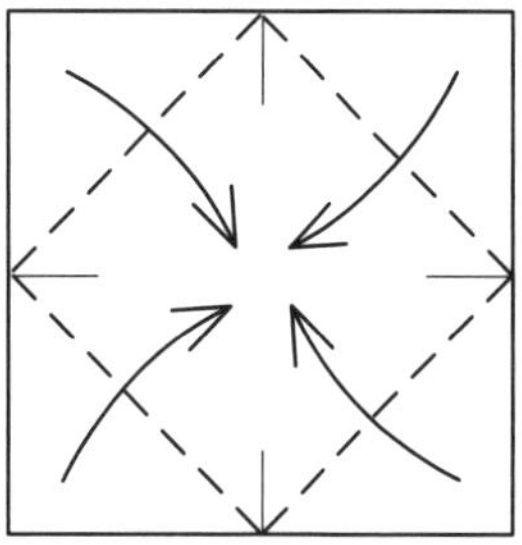

3

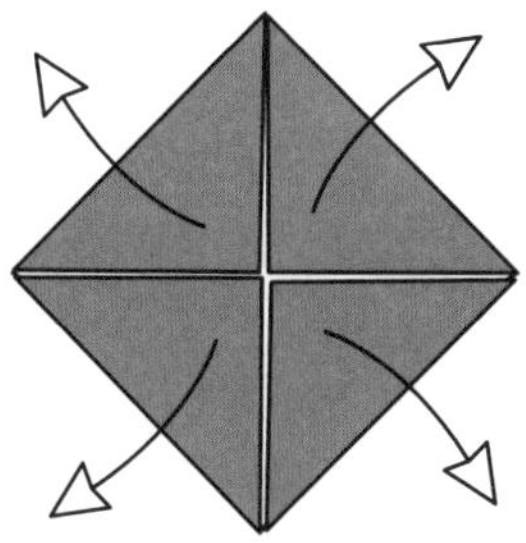

Unfold.

4

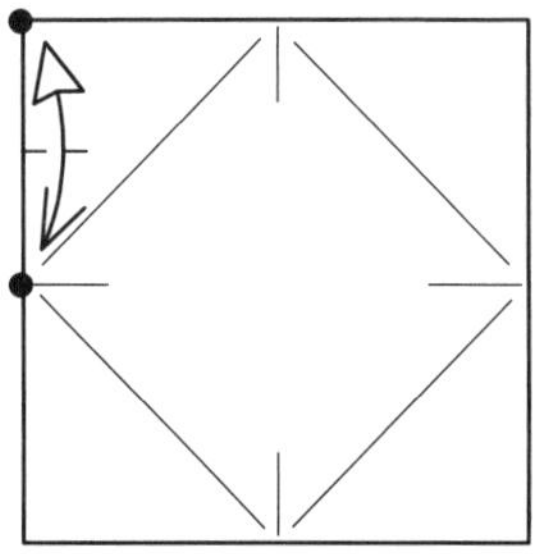

Fold and unfold on the left.

5

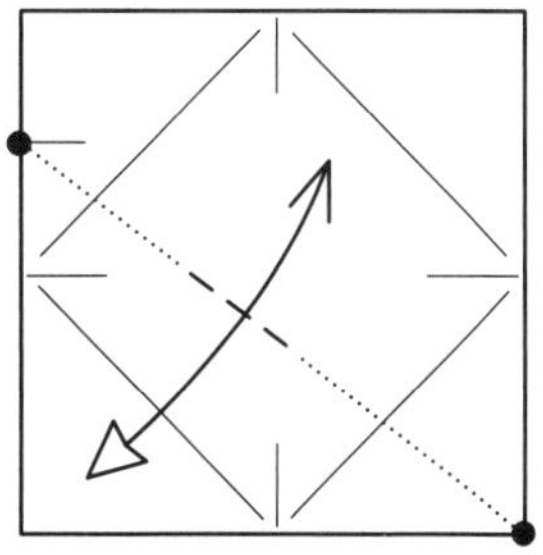

Fold and unfold in the center.

6

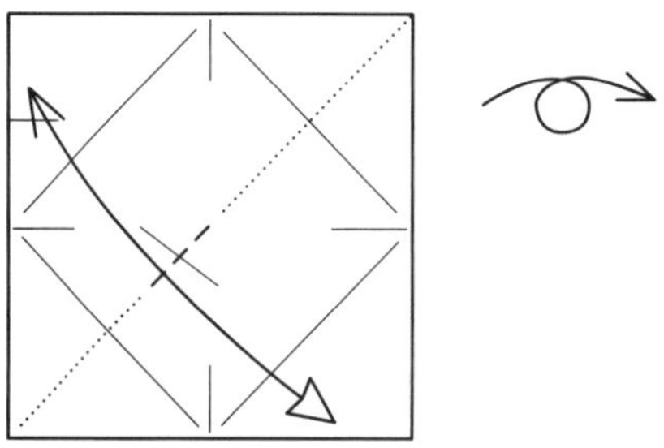

Fold and unfold in the center.

7

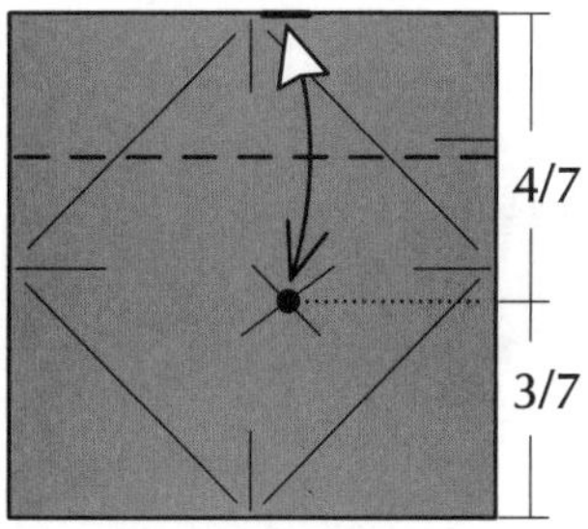

Fold and unfold. The paper is divided into 3/7 and 4/7.

8

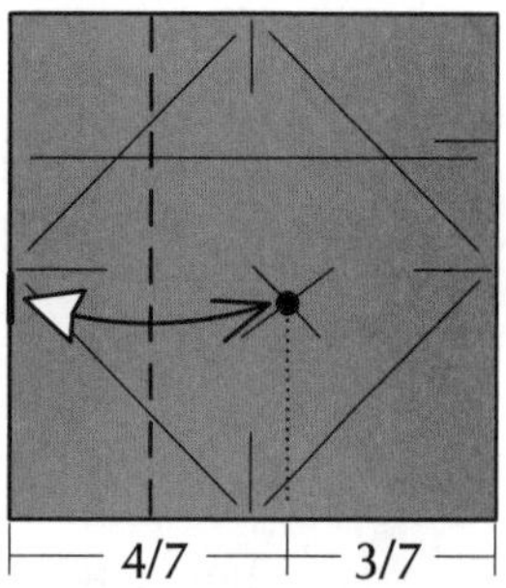

Fold and unfold.

9

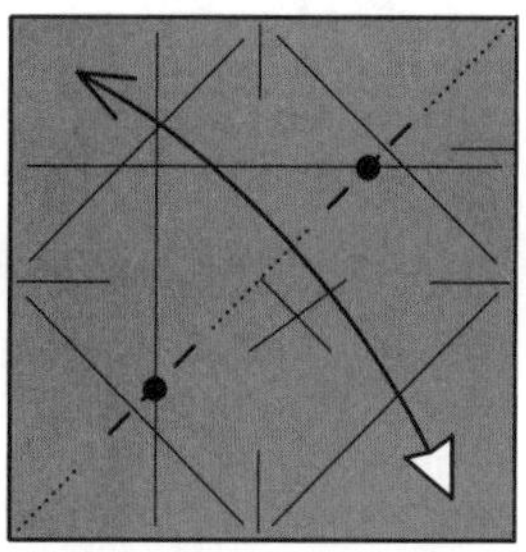

Fold and unfold only on the vertical and horizontal lines.

10

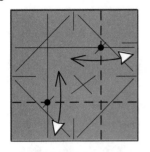

Fold and unfold. Rotate.

11

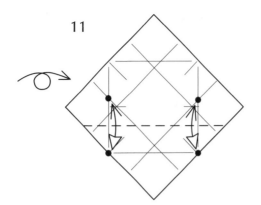

Fold and unfold.
Rotate 90°.

12

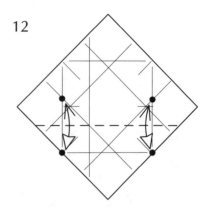

Repeat step 11
three more times.

13

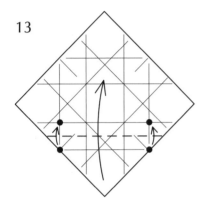

14

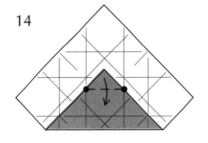

15

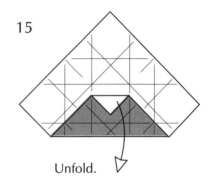

Unfold.

16

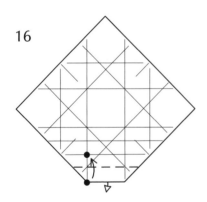

17

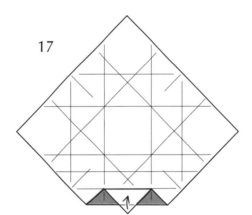

18

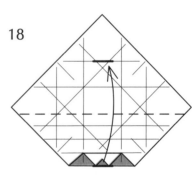

Bring the edge
to the line.

19

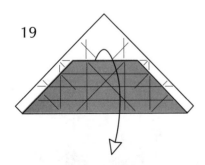

Unfold everything.

20

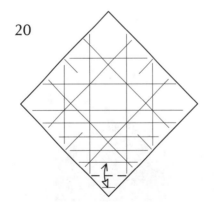

Unfold and unfold along
the crease. Rotate 90°.

21

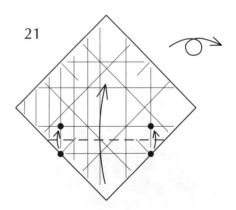

Repeat steps 13–20
three more times.

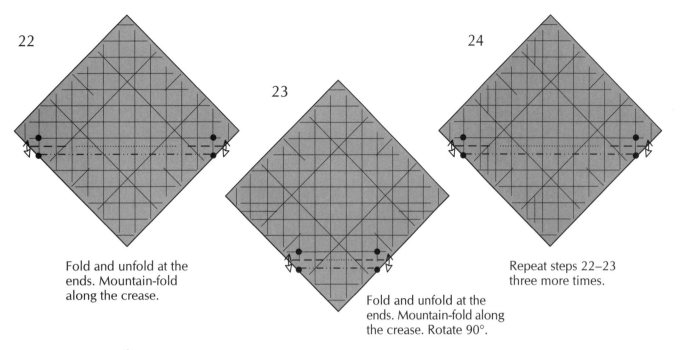

22 Fold and unfold at the ends. Mountain-fold along the crease.

23 Fold and unfold at the ends. Mountain-fold along the crease. Rotate 90°.

24 Repeat steps 22–23 three more times.

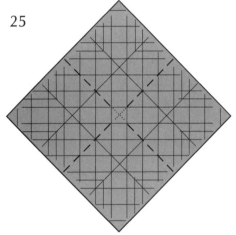

25 Fold and unfold in half, along partial creases, but do not crease in the center. Rotate.

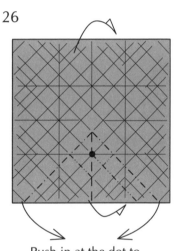

26 Push in at the dot to form a sunken triangle.

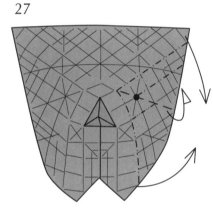

27 Repeat step 26 three more times.

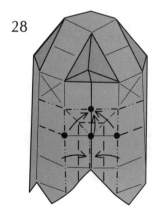

28 Collapse along the creases so the four dots meet.

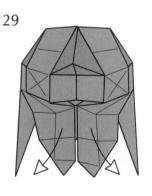

29 Unfold back to step 28. Rotate 90°.

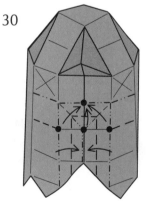

30 Repeat steps 28–29 three more times.

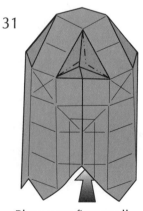

31 Place your fingers all the way inside to flatten the sunken triangle.

32

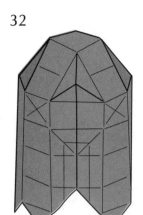

Repeat step 31 three more times.

33

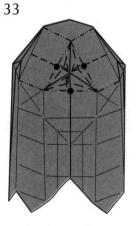

The dots will meet. Repeat three more times.

34

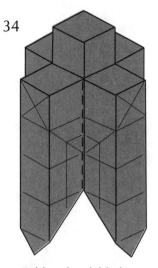

Fold and unfold along the edge. Repeat three more times.

35

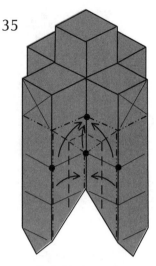

Refold along the creases. Repeat three more times.

36

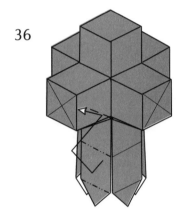

Fold and unfold along the creases. Repeat three more times. Rotate the top to the bottom.

37

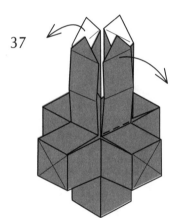

Spread two opposite flaps.

38

Fold the tip down on one side.

39

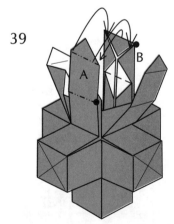

Region A will tuck into the pockets of B, so B will cover A. The dots will meet.

40

Repeat steps 38–39 to close the model. Rotate the top to the bottom.

41

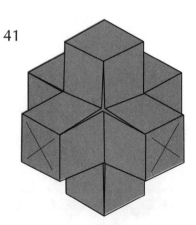

Cubicles

Triangular Troublewit

Origami troublewits are models based on accordian-style folds. I will present a towering triangular, square, and pentagonal troublewit. These are good examples of dividing the paper into *n*ths.

For this triangular troublewit, the paper is divided into 9ths.

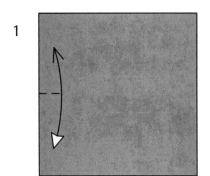

1

Fold and unfold on the left.

2

Bring the bottom right corner to the top and the bottom edge to the dot. Crease on the left.

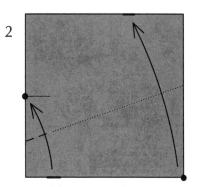

3

Unfold.

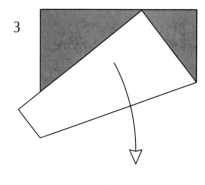

4

2/9

The 2/9 mark is found. Fold up so the dots meet.

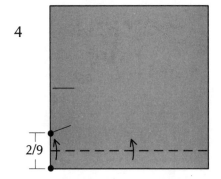

5

Fold in half.

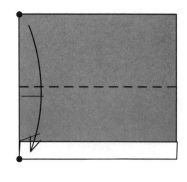

6

Unfold.

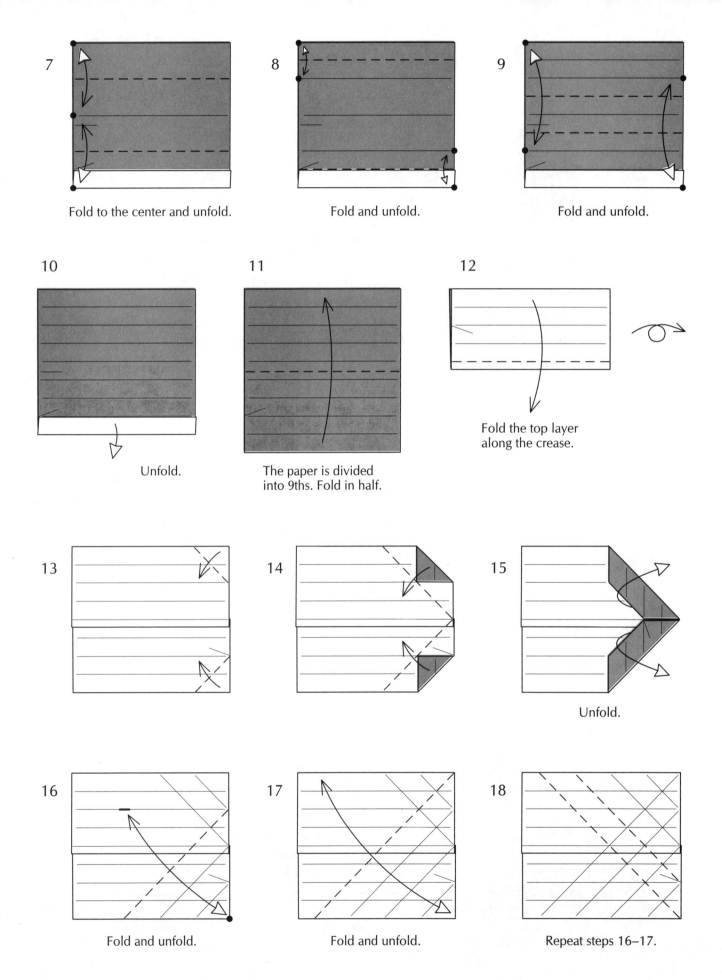

7 Fold to the center and unfold.

8 Fold and unfold.

9 Fold and unfold.

10 Unfold.

11 The paper is divided into 9ths. Fold in half.

12 Fold the top layer along the crease.

13

14

15 Unfold.

16 Fold and unfold.

17 Fold and unfold.

18 Repeat steps 16–17.

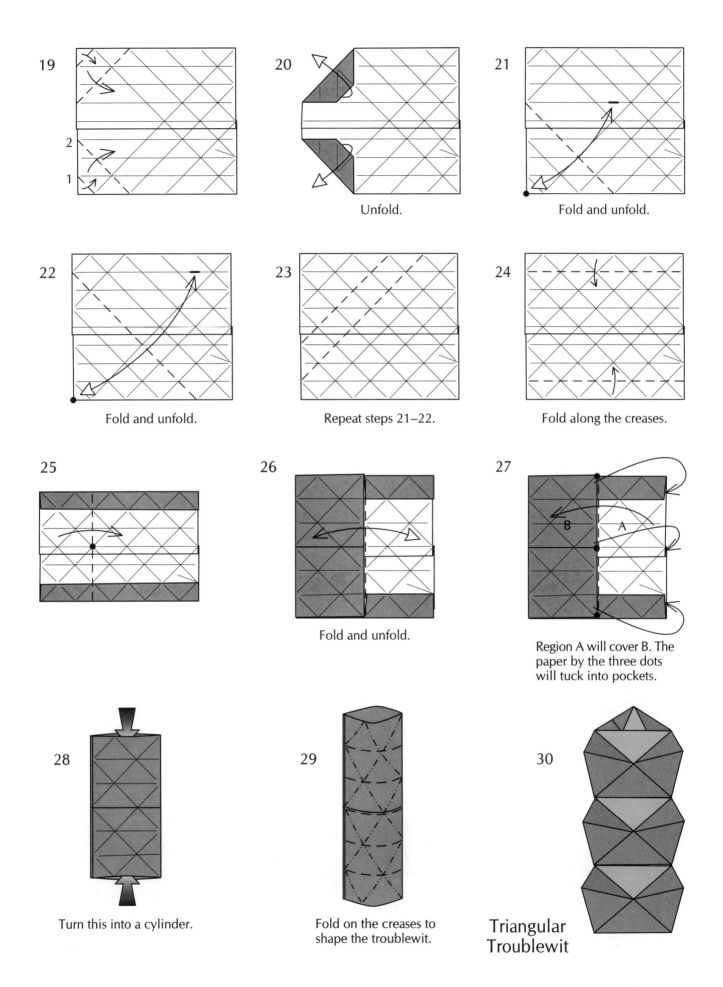

19

20

Unfold.

21

Fold and unfold.

22

Fold and unfold.

23

Repeat steps 21–22.

24

Fold along the creases.

25

26

Fold and unfold.

27

Region A will cover B. The paper by the three dots will tuck into pockets.

28

Turn this into a cylinder.

29

Fold on the creases to shape the troublewit.

30

Triangular Troublewit

Square Troublewit

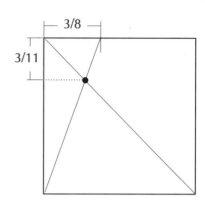

The paper is divided into 11ths to fold the square troublewit.

1
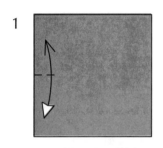

Fold and unfold
on the left.

2
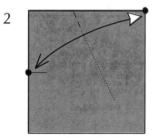

Fold and unfold
at the top.

3

Fold and unfold
at the top, center.

4
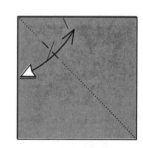

Fold and unfold by
the intersection.

5
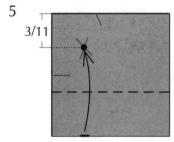

The 3/11 mark is found.
Fold the edge to the dot.

6
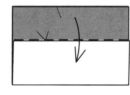

7
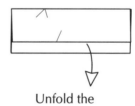

Unfold the
middle layer.

8
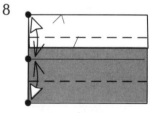

Fold to the center
and unfold.

9
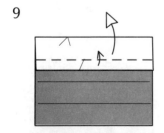

Fold along the crease,
then unfold the rest.

10
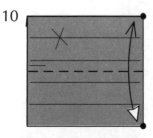

Fold in half
and unfold.

11
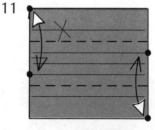

Fold and unfold.

12
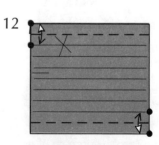

Fold and unfold.

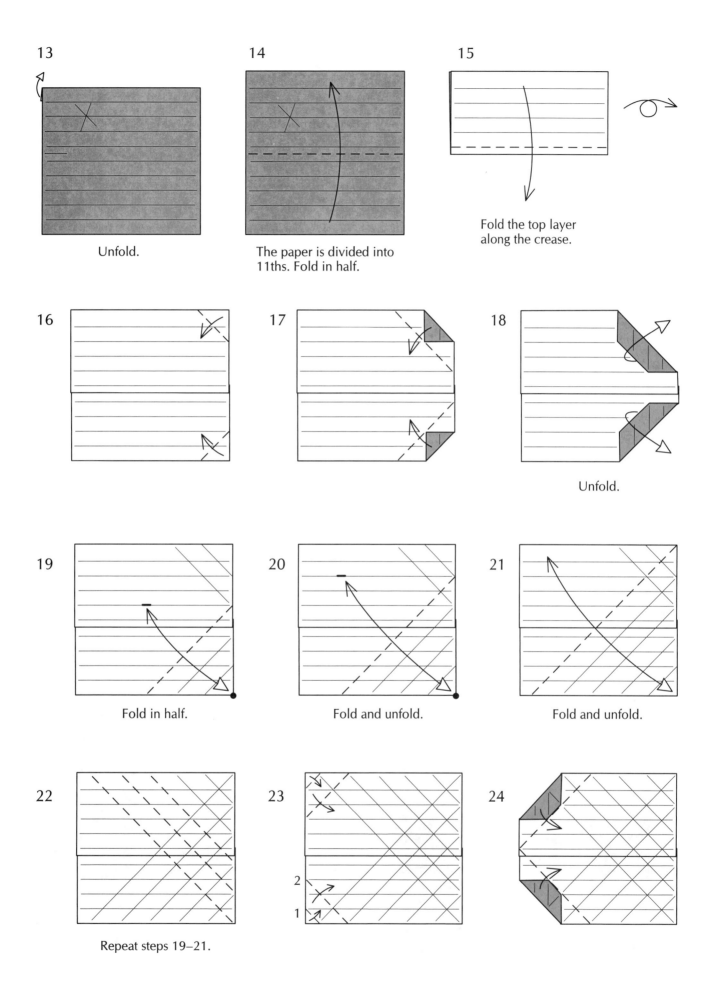

13

Unfold.

14

The paper is divided into 11ths. Fold in half.

15

Fold the top layer along the crease.

16

17

18

Unfold.

19

Fold in half.

20

Fold and unfold.

21

Fold and unfold.

22

Repeat steps 19–21.

23

2

1

24

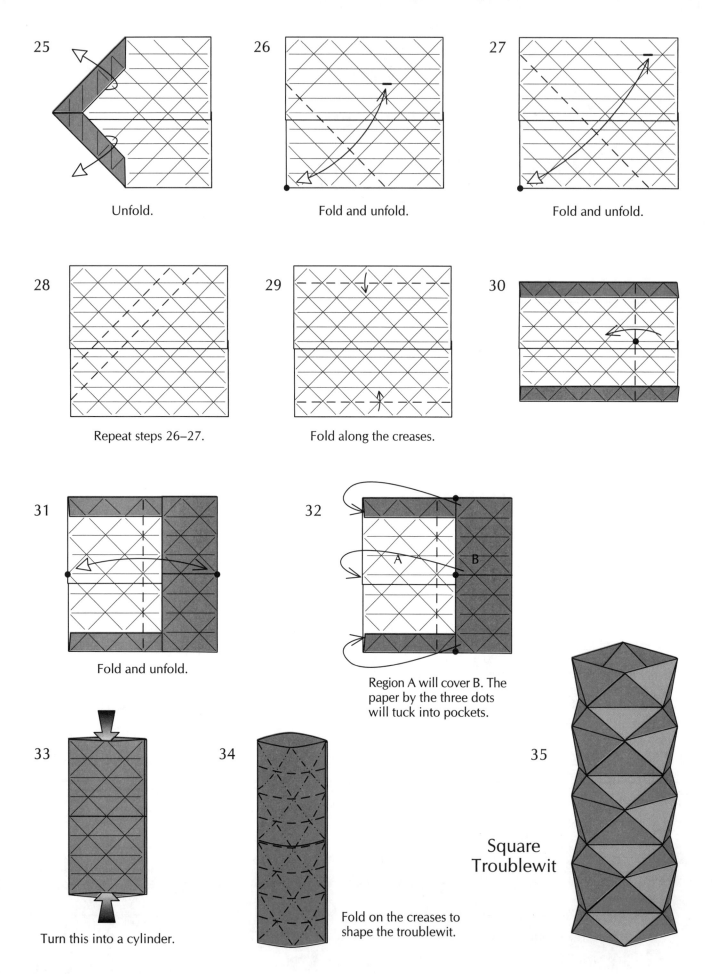

25 Unfold.

26 Fold and unfold.

27 Fold and unfold.

28 Repeat steps 26–27.

29 Fold along the creases.

30

31 Fold and unfold.

32 Region A will cover B. The paper by the three dots will tuck into pockets.

33 Turn this into a cylinder.

34 Fold on the creases to shape the troublewit.

35 Square Troublewit

Pentagonal Troublewit

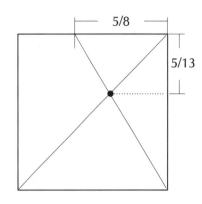

The paper is divided into 13ths to fold the pentagonal troublewit.

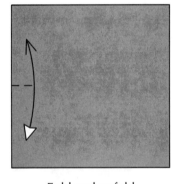

1

Fold and unfold
on the left.

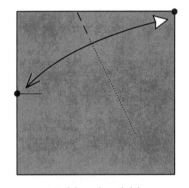

2

Fold and unfold
at the top.

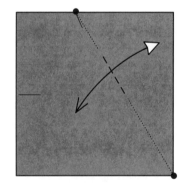

3

Fold and unfold
at the top, center.

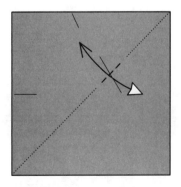

4

Fold and unfold by
the intersection.

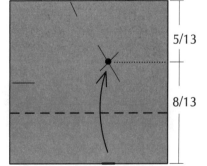

5

The 5/13 mark is found.
Fold the edge to the dot.

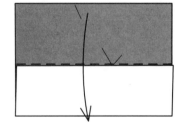

6

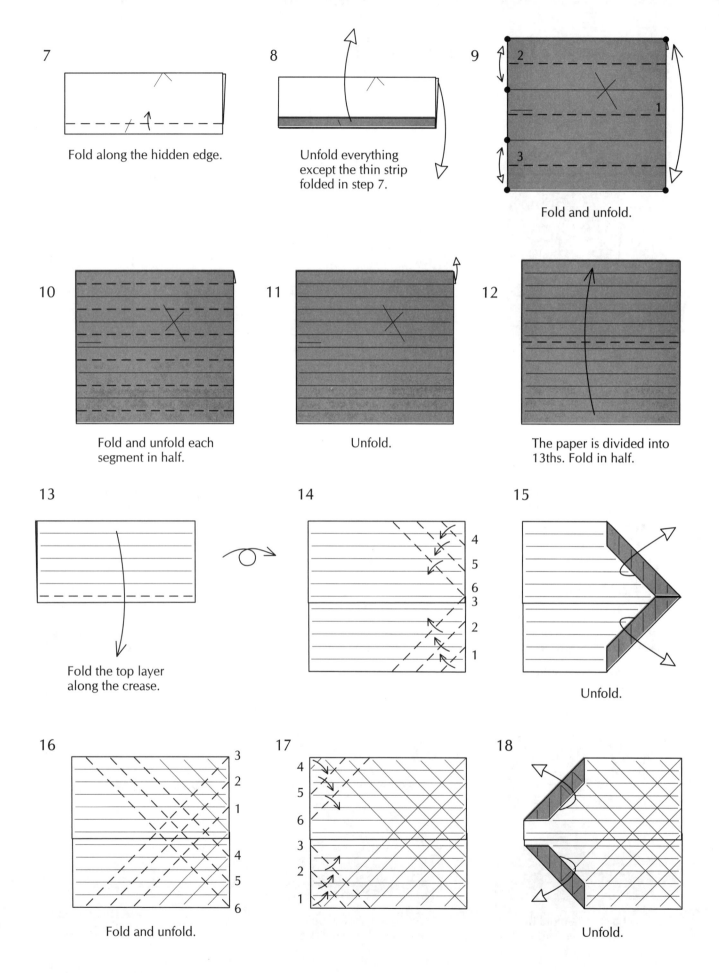

7

Fold along the hidden edge.

8

Unfold everything
except the thin strip
folded in step 7.

9

2

1

3

Fold and unfold.

10

Fold and unfold each
segment in half.

11

Unfold.

12

The paper is divided into
13ths. Fold in half.

13

Fold the top layer
along the crease.

14

4
5
6
3
2
1

15

Unfold.

16

3
2
1
4
5
6

Fold and unfold.

17

4
5
6
3
2
1

18

Unfold.

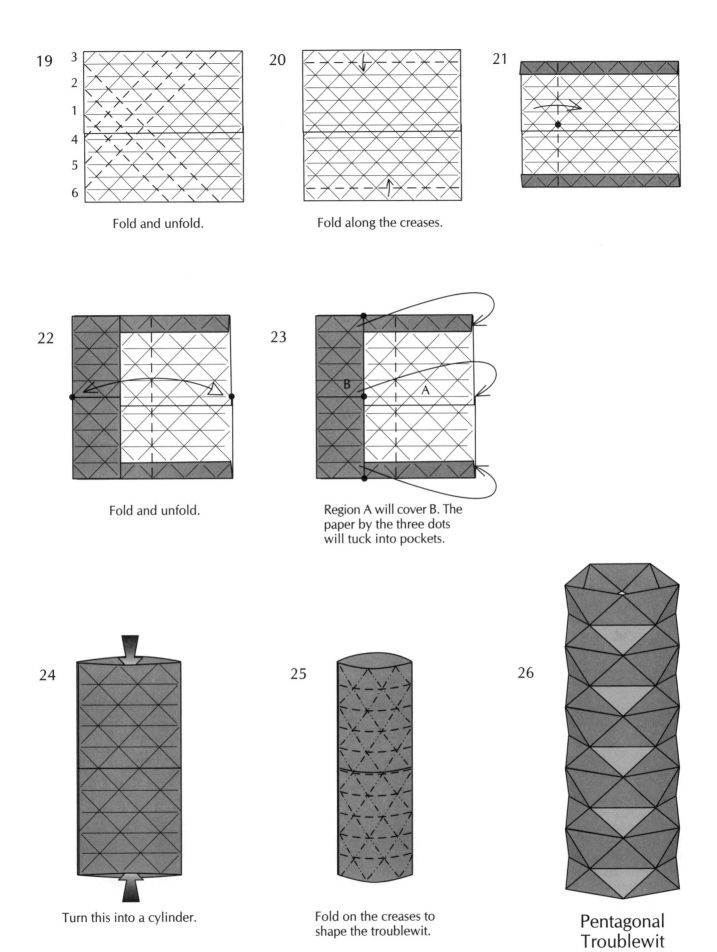

19

3
2
1
4
5
6

Fold and unfold.

20

Fold along the creases.

21

22

Fold and unfold.

23

Region A will cover B. The
paper by the three dots
will tuck into pockets.

B

A

24

Turn this into a cylinder.

25

Fold on the creases to
shape the troublewit.

26

Pentagonal
Troublewit

Chess Boards

Origami chess boards are extreme examples of using origami for its color effect. For an $n \times n$ board, it doesn't take long for the model to become complex and challenging to develop or fold. Though the standard board is 8×8, we can consider the $n \times n$ board for origami.

The chess boards come in two styles. One is called fuzzy, where the small squares have exposed diagonals, and the other is clean, where each square is a solid panel. The fuzzy boards are easier to fold and larger than the clean ones.

In designing these chess boards, I am interested in
1. The paper is used efficiently to make the board as large as possible.
2. The folding is not too complex, and can be diagrammed.
3. The finished model holds together well.
4. Clean is preferable to fuzzy, but not at the expense of 1, 2, 3 above.
5. The board should also be a chess table, if possible.

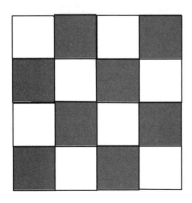

4 × 4 Clean Chess Board

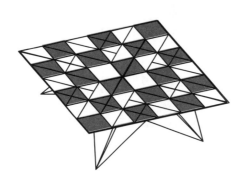

6 × 6 Chess Table

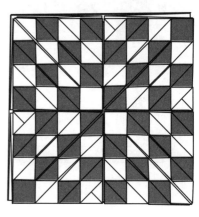

8 × 8 Fuzzy Chess Board

Size of Chess Board

Assume each board is folded from a 1×1 square. For a given $n \times n$ board, a conjectured largest size ($s \times s$) is given by the formula, for $n < 9$:

n even

$s = 2/3$ for $n = 2$

$s = 2/n$ for $n > 2$

n odd

$s = 2n/(n^2 + 1)$

n	s
1	1
2	2/3
3	3/5
4	1/2
5	5/13
6	1/3
7	7/25
8	1/4

Here is a table which shows the size of each chess board in this collection. Assume each model is folded from a 1×1 square sheet of paper. The first few are clean, the more difficult ones are fuzzy. Not all the boards are the most efficient in size. Though I had worked some of them out, the slightly smaller versions were better to fold.

n	s	style
1	1	clean
2	2/3	clean
3	3/5	clean
4	2/5	clean
5	5/13	fuzzy
6	1/4	fuzzy
7	7/27	fuzzy
8	2/9	fuzzy

1 × 1 Chess Board

This is certainly not a very interesting one to fold. Can it even be considered origami? Still, it is fun to include and exhibit with the set of chess boards.

All the other chess boards are compared to this; in size (the 3 × 3 board is 3/5 the size of the 1 × 1 board), thickness, number of folds away from it, among others.

Traditional Japanese origami had no care about the shape or color effect. In the 1800's, Friedrich Frobel from Germany started the kindergarten movement. Around 1880 he developed origami paper as square sheets that were used to teach geometry to children. The Japanese adopted this movement, and developed origami paper with a solid color on one side and white on the other.

For a long time, many models used multiple squares, other geometric shapes, or cuts. In the progression of origami development, there became a standard where models were each folded from a single uncut square, which I helped pioneer. By using origami paper, the models used the effects of the two colors, or at least showed the model in the solid color.

Origami chess boards are extreme examples of using origami for its color effect. For an $n \times n$ board, it doesn't take long for the model to become complex and a challenge to develop or fold. This 1 × 1 board is clean, optimal in size, and minimal in number of folds!

2 × 2 Chess Board

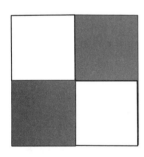

The length of the side of this 2 × 2 chess board is 2/3 that of the original square, shown on the right. The white squares in the right figure show the location of the white squares when folded. The dark squares show the location of the dark squares. The gray represents the hidden part.

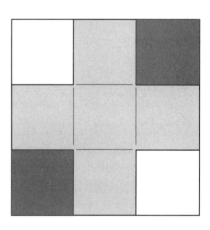

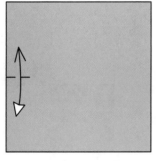

1

Fold and unfold on the left.

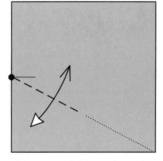

2

Fold and unfold on the left.

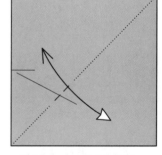

3

Fold and unfold at the intersection. Rotate.

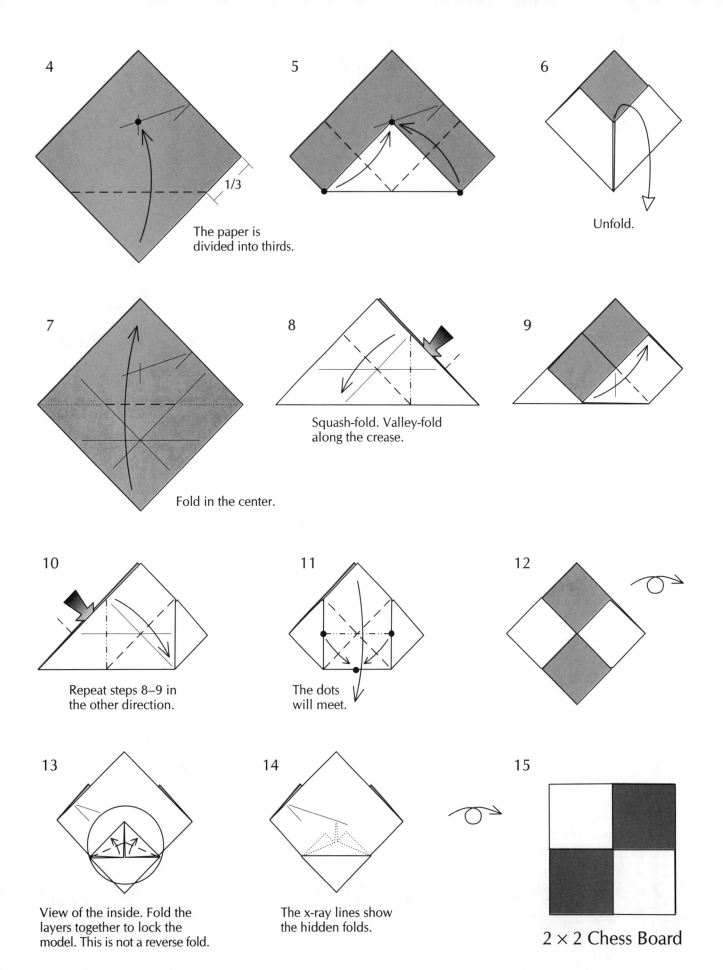

4

1/3

5

The paper is
divided into thirds.

6

Unfold.

7

Fold in the center.

8

Squash-fold. Valley-fold
along the crease.

9

10

Repeat steps 8–9 in
the other direction.

11

The dots
will meet.

12

13

View of the inside. Fold the
layers together to lock the
model. This is not a reverse fold.

14

The x-ray lines show
the hidden folds.

15

2 × 2 Chess Board

3 × 3 Chess Board

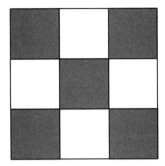

The length of the side of this 3 × 3 chess board is 3/5 that of the original square, as shown on the right. You can follow which parts of the square paper becomes the visible parts represented in the model. This model uses square symmetry.

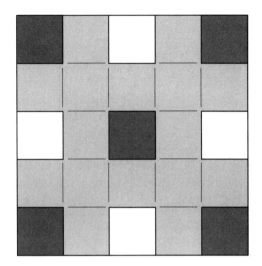

1

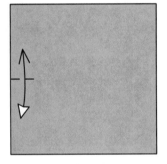

Fold and unfold on the left.

2

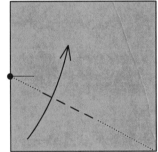

Crease in the center.

3

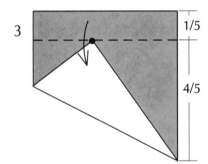

1/5

4/5

The paper is divided into fifths.

4

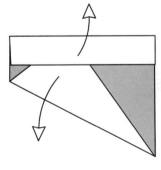

Unfold.

5

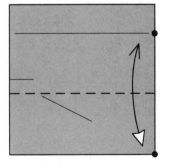

Fold and unfold.

6

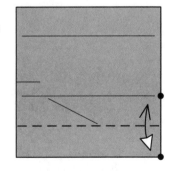

Fold and unfold.

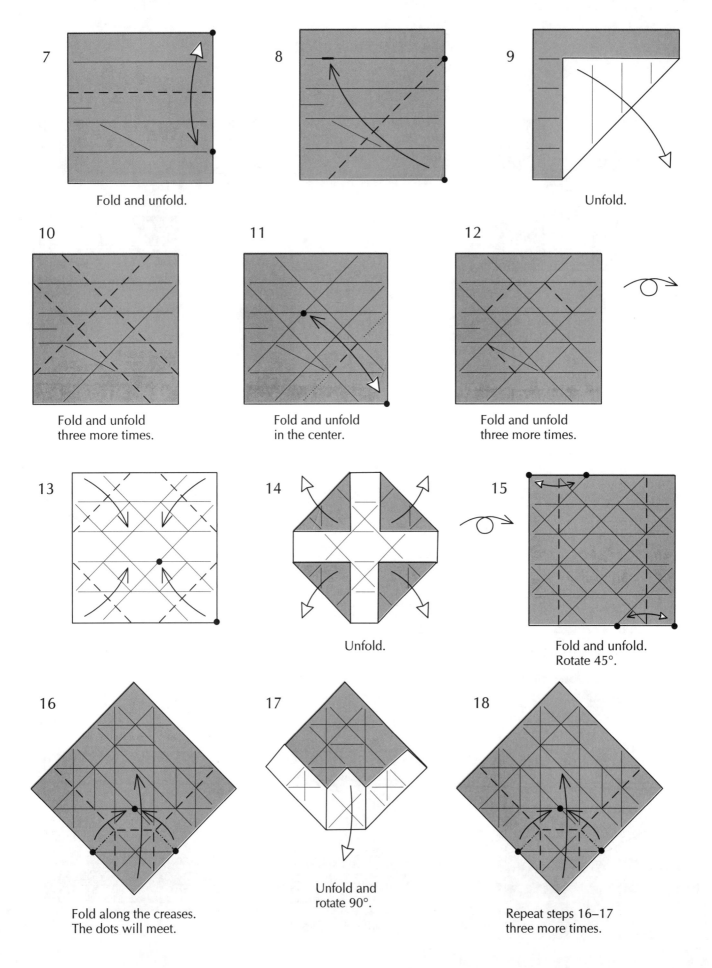

7 Fold and unfold.

8

9 Unfold.

10 Fold and unfold three more times.

11 Fold and unfold in the center.

12 Fold and unfold three more times.

13 Fold along the creases. The dots will meet.

14 Unfold.

15 Fold and unfold. Rotate 45°.

16 Fold along the creases. The dots will meet.

17 Unfold and rotate 90°.

18 Repeat steps 16–17 three more times.

19

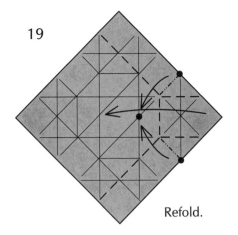

Refold.

20

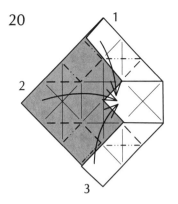

1
2
3

Continue refolding in the order
shown. Each corner, in order,
will cover the center.

21

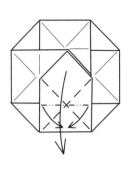

Fold along the creases.

22

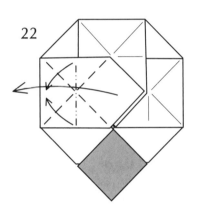

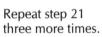

Repeat step 21
three more times.

23

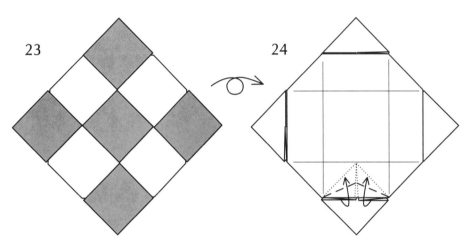

24

Fold the inside layers
together to lock the model.

25

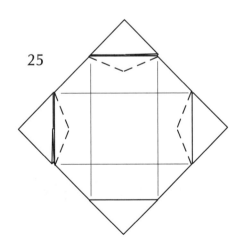

Repeat step 24
three more times.

26

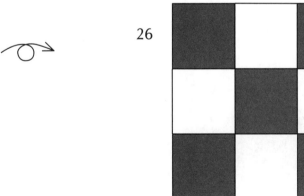

3 × 3 Chess Board

4 × 4 Chess Board

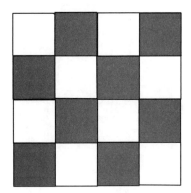

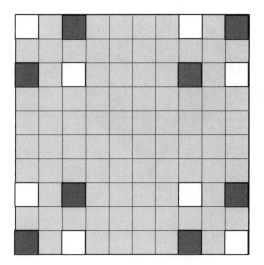

The length of the side of this 4 × 4 chess board is 2/5 that of the original square, as shown on the right. You can follow which parts of the square paper becomes the visible parts represented in the model.

1

Fold and unfold on the left.

2

Crease on the left.

3

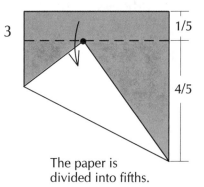

1/5

4/5

The paper is divided into fifths.

4

Unfold.

5

Fold and unfold.

6

Fold and unfold.

7

Fold and unfold.

8

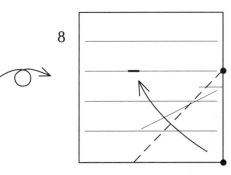

9

Unfold.

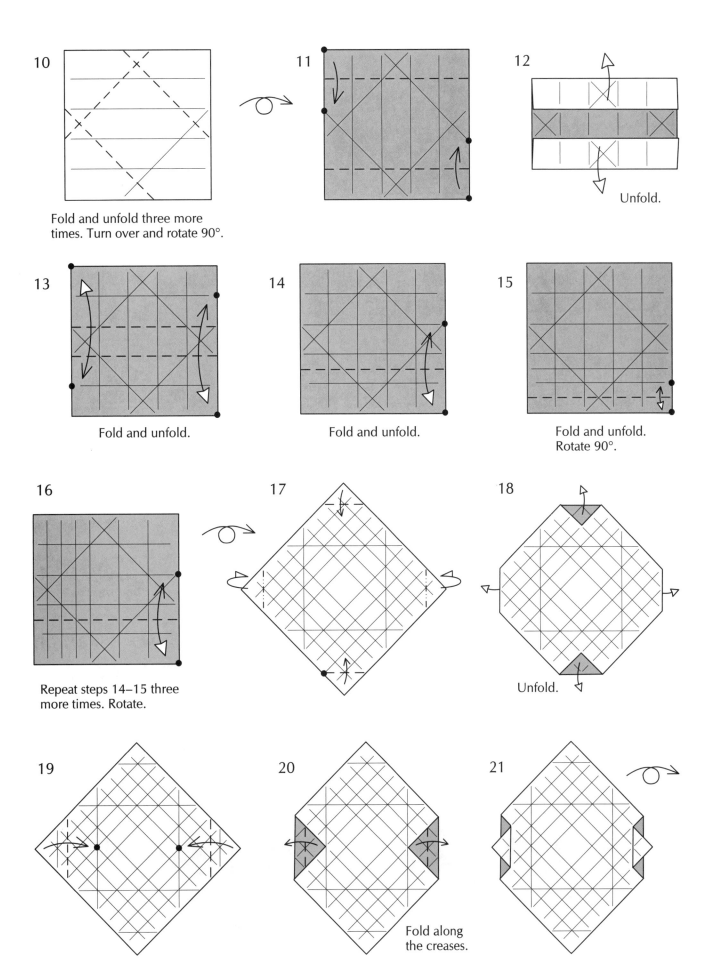

10 Fold and unfold three more times. Turn over and rotate 90°.

12 Unfold.

13 Fold and unfold.

14 Fold and unfold.

15 Fold and unfold. Rotate 90°.

16 Repeat steps 14–15 three more times. Rotate.

18 Unfold.

20 Fold along the creases.

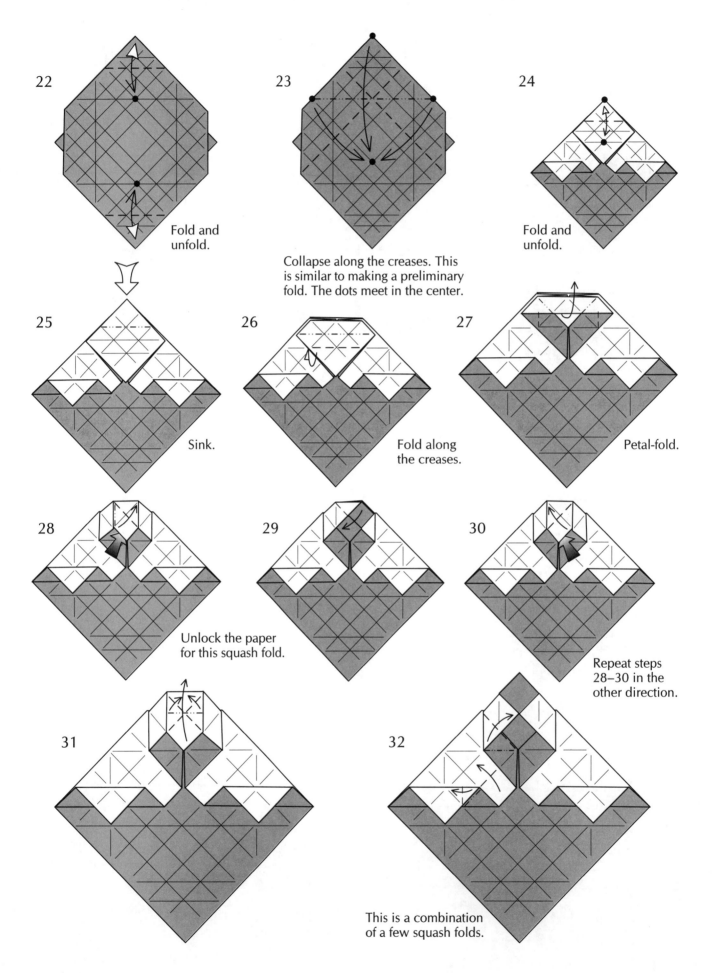

22   Fold and unfold.

23   Collapse along the creases. This is similar to making a preliminary fold. The dots meet in the center.

24   Fold and unfold.

25   Sink.

26   Fold along the creases.

27   Petal-fold.

28   Unlock the paper for this squash fold.

29

30   Repeat steps 28–30 in the other direction.

31

32   This is a combination of a few squash folds.

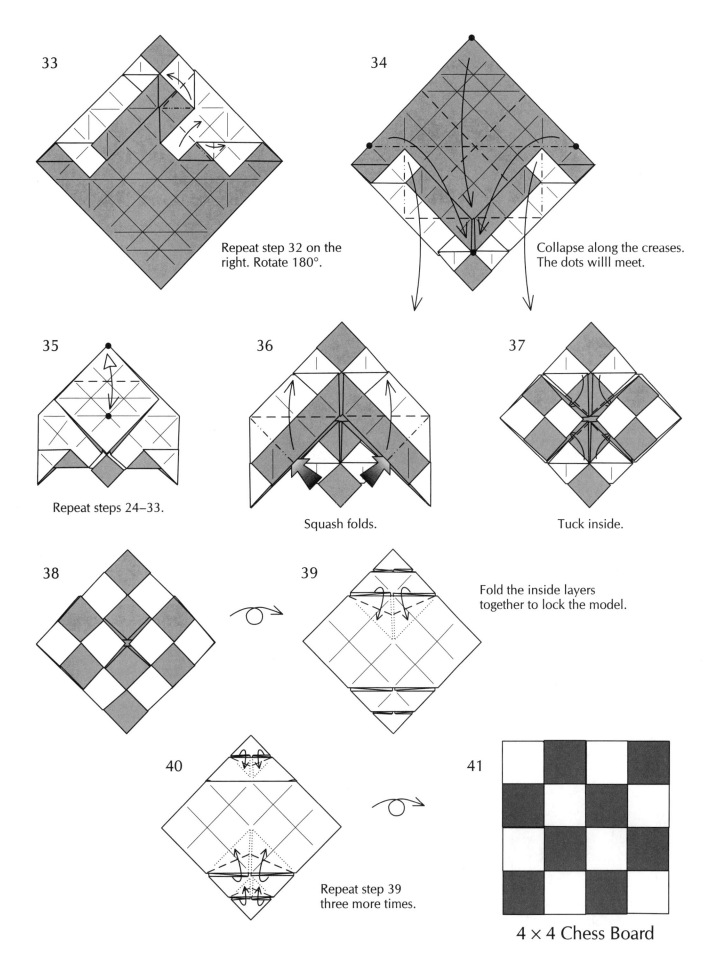

33

Repeat step 32 on the right. Rotate 180°.

34

Collapse along the creases. The dots willl meet.

35

Repeat steps 24–33.

36

Squash folds.

37

Tuck inside.

38

39

Fold the inside layers together to lock the model.

40

Repeat step 39 three more times.

41

4 × 4 Chess Board

4 × 4 Chess Board 49

5 × 5 Chess Board

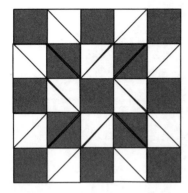

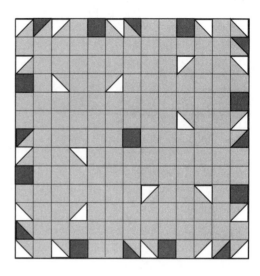

This is a "fuzzy" board since some of the squares have exposed diagonals. The length of the side of this 5 × 5 chess board is 5/13 that of the original square, as shown on the right. I suspect the pattern on the right to be more for entertainment than analysis. The model uses square symmetry.

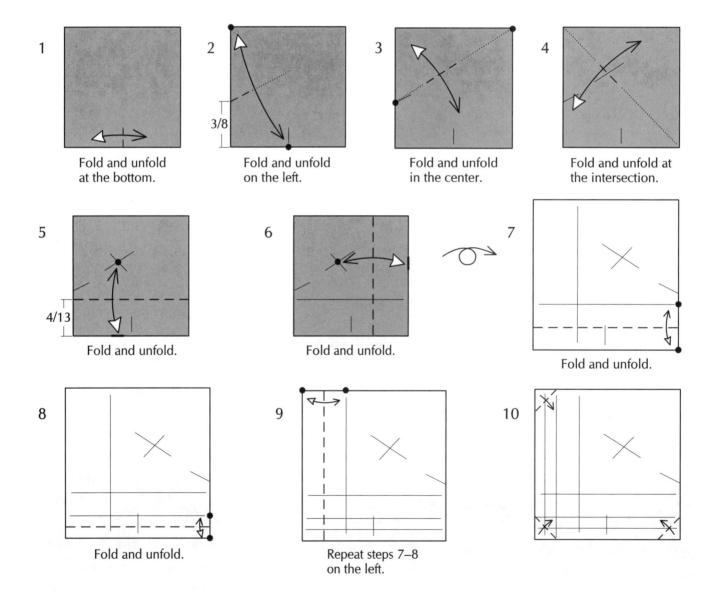

1   Fold and unfold at the bottom.

2   3/8   Fold and unfold on the left.

3   Fold and unfold in the center.

4   Fold and unfold at the intersection.

5   4/13   Fold and unfold.

6   Fold and unfold.

7   Fold and unfold.

8   Fold and unfold.

9   Repeat steps 7–8 on the left.

10

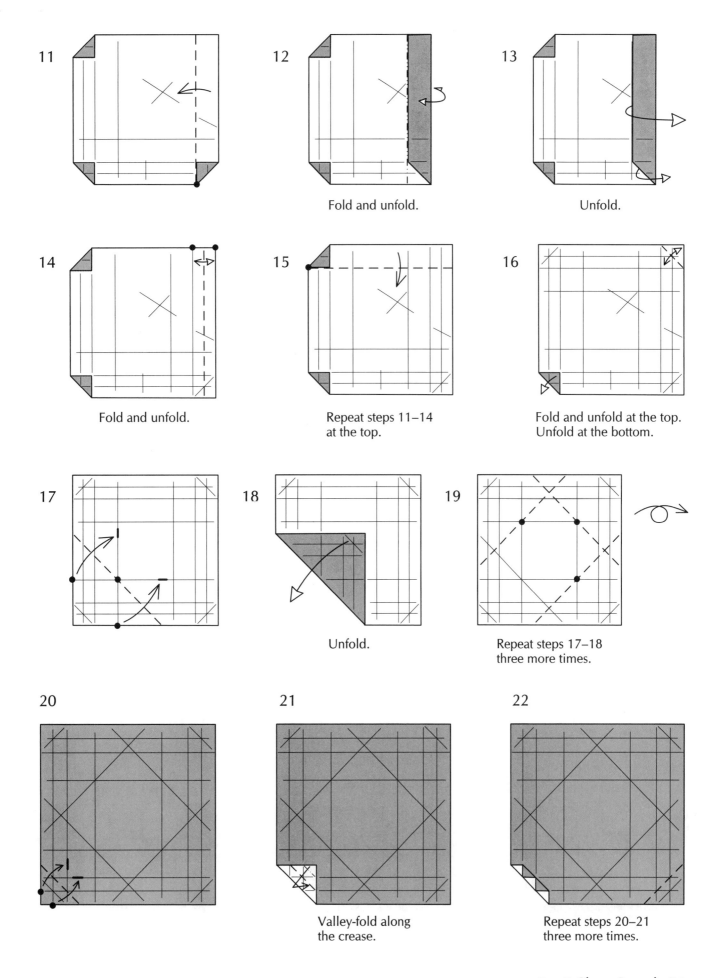

11

12

Fold and unfold.

13

Unfold.

14

Fold and unfold.

15

Repeat steps 11–14
at the top.

16

Fold and unfold at the top.
Unfold at the bottom.

17

18

Unfold.

19

Repeat steps 17–18
three more times.

20

21

Valley-fold along
the crease.

22

Repeat steps 20–21
three more times.

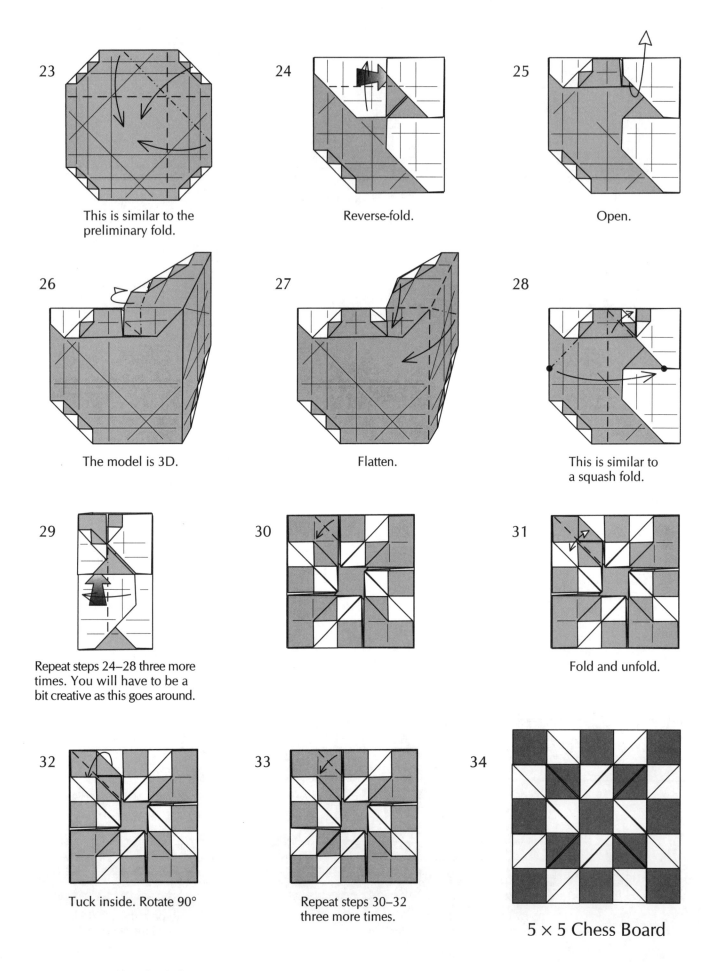

23

This is similar to the preliminary fold.

24

Reverse-fold.

25

Open.

26

The model is 3D.

27

Flatten.

28

This is similar to a squash fold.

29

Repeat steps 24–28 three more times. You will have to be a bit creative as this goes around.

30

31

Fold and unfold.

32

Tuck inside. Rotate 90°

33

Repeat steps 30–32 three more times.

34

5 × 5 Chess Board

6 × 6 Chess Board & Table

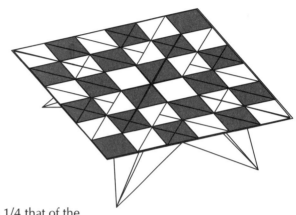

The length of the side of this 6 × 6 chess board is 1/4 that of the original square. The most efficient one in size would have a length of 1/3. However, this model has several good attributes: it can also be a chess table, is easier with fewer steps than the most efficient version, and is similar in folding to the 8 × 8 board.

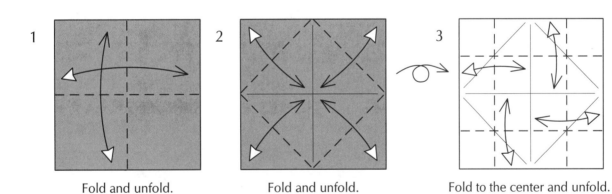

1 Fold and unfold.

2 Fold and unfold.

3 Fold to the center and unfold.

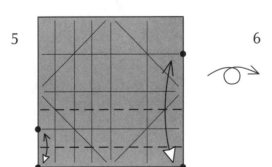

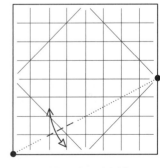

4 Fold and unfold to divide into eigths. Rotate 90°.

5 Repeat step 4 three more times.

6 Fold and unfold by the intersection.

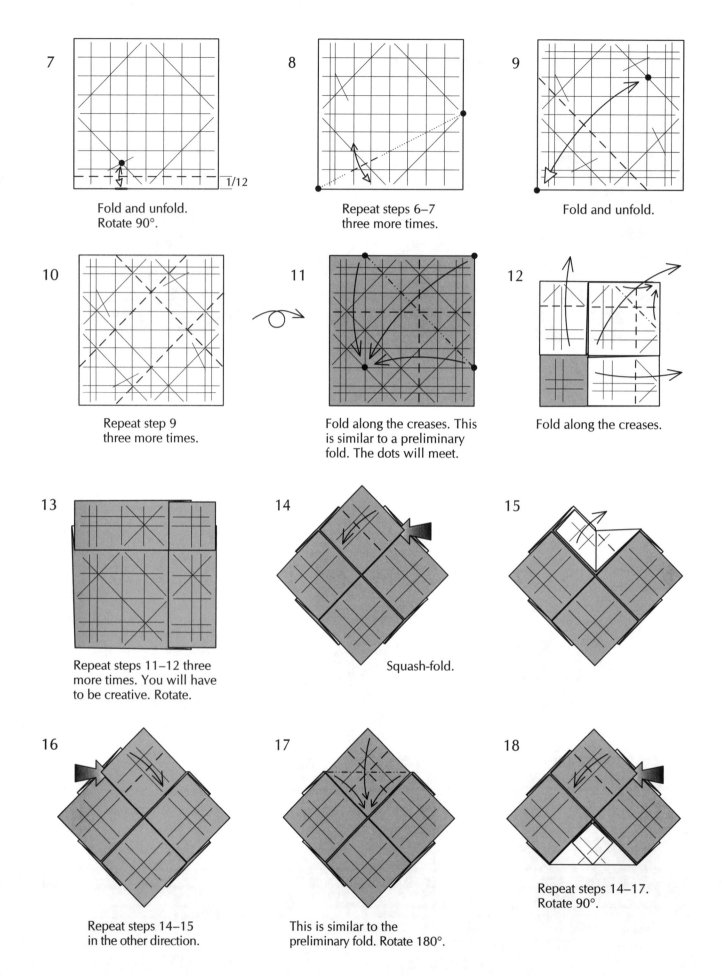

7 Fold and unfold. Rotate 90°.

1/12

8 Repeat steps 6–7 three more times.

9 Fold and unfold.

10 Repeat step 9 three more times.

11 Fold along the creases. This is similar to a preliminary fold. The dots will meet.

12 Fold along the creases.

13 Repeat steps 11–12 three more times. You will have to be creative. Rotate.

14 Squash-fold.

15

16 Repeat steps 14–15 in the other direction.

17 This is similar to the preliminary fold. Rotate 180°.

18 Repeat steps 14–17. Rotate 90°.

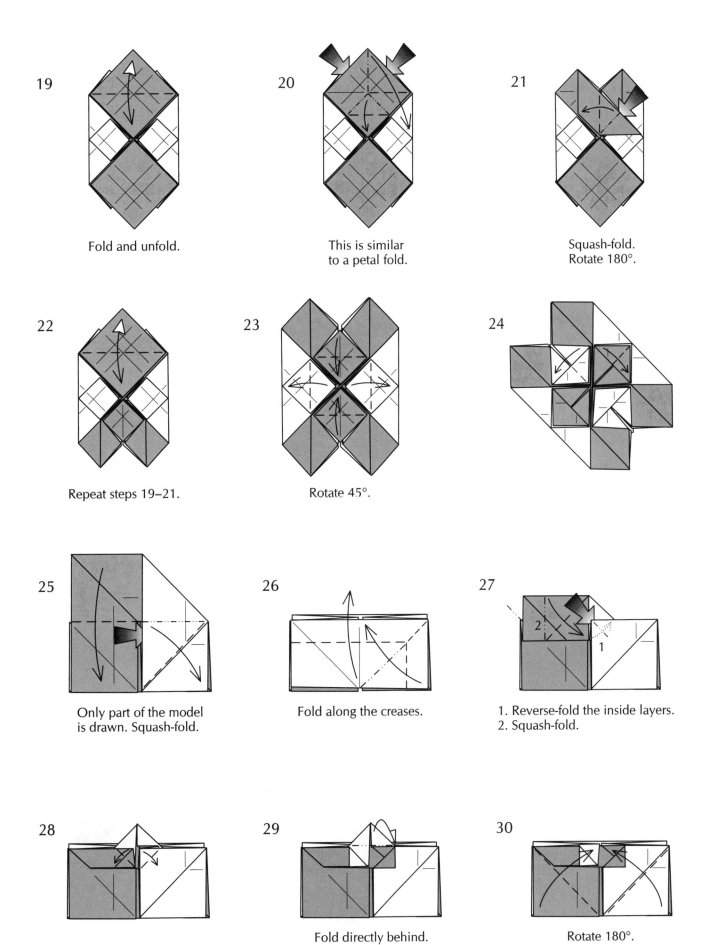

19   Fold and unfold.

20   This is similar to a petal fold.

21   Squash-fold. Rotate 180°.

22   Repeat steps 19–21.

23   Rotate 45°.

24

25   Only part of the model is drawn. Squash-fold.

26   Fold along the creases.

27   1. Reverse-fold the inside layers.
2. Squash-fold.

28

29   Fold directly behind.

30   Rotate 180°.

31

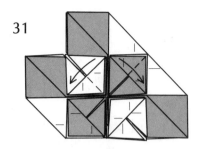

Repeat steps 24–30.

32

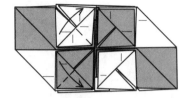

Repeat steps 24–31 in the opposite direction.

33

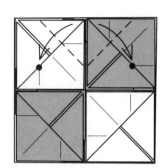

34

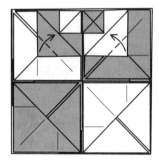

35

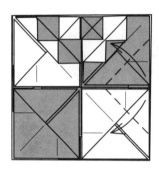

Repeat steps 33–34 three more times.

36

6 × 6 Chess Board

37

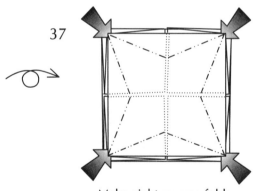

Make eight reverse folds.

38

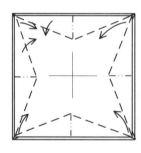

Make the legs 3D.

39

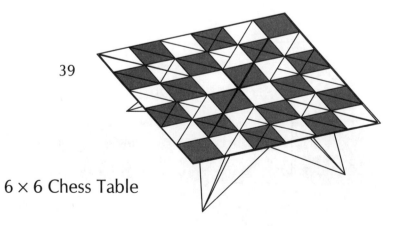

6 × 6 Chess Table

7 × 7 Chess Board & Table

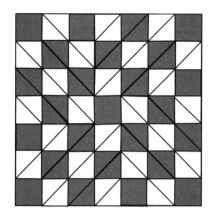

The length of the side of this 7 × 7 chess board is 7/27 (or ≈ .259) that of the original square. This board can also become a table.

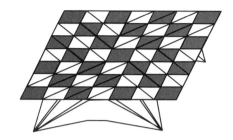

1
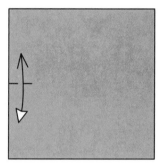

Fold and unfold
on the left.

2

Fold and unfold
on the left.

3
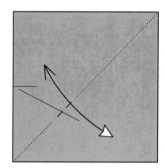

Fold and unfold at
the intersection.

4
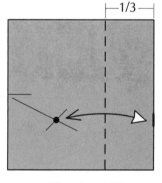

├─1/3─┤

Fold and unfold.

5
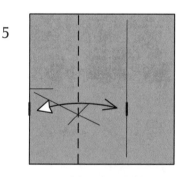

Fold and unfold.

6
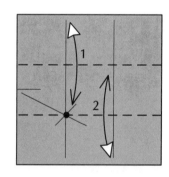

1

2

Fold and unfold.

7

2/9

Fold and unfold
on the left.

8

Fold and unfold.
Rotate 90°.

9
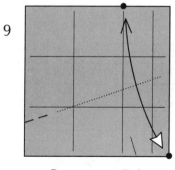

Repeat steps 7–8
three more times.

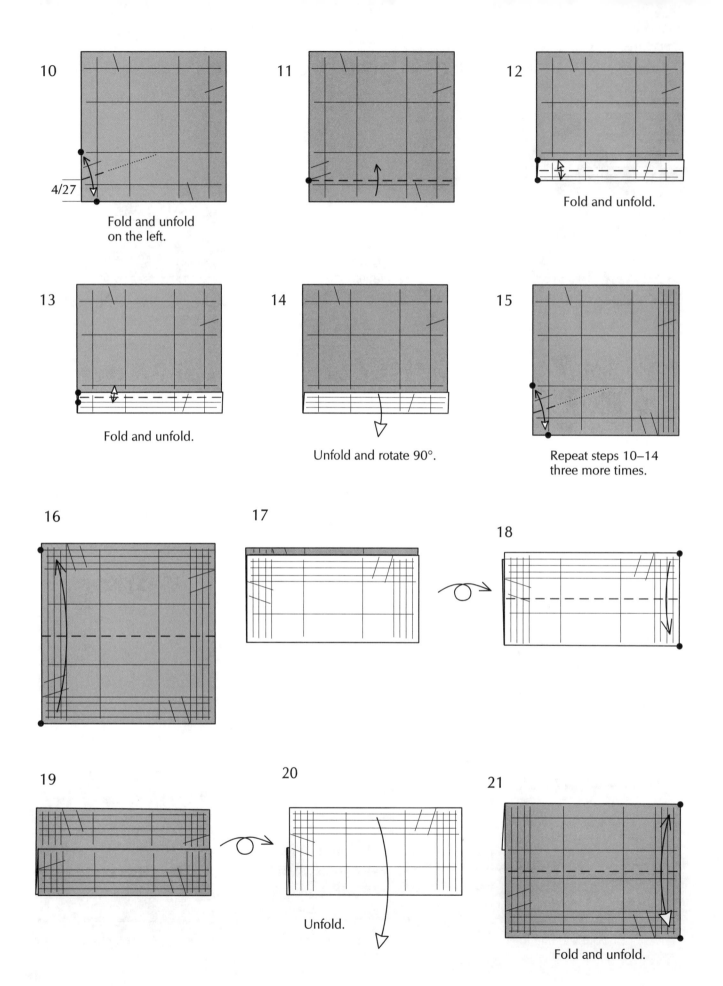

10

4/27

Fold and unfold
on the left.

11

12

Fold and unfold.

13

Fold and unfold.

14

Unfold and rotate 90°.

15

Repeat steps 10–14
three more times.

16

17

18

19

20

Unfold.

21

Fold and unfold.

22

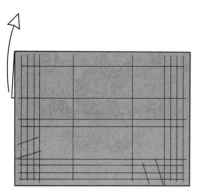

Unfold and rotate 90°.

23

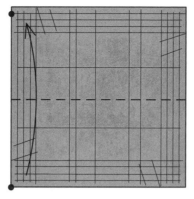

Repeat steps 16–22
three more times.

24

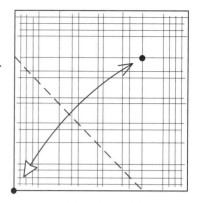

Fold and unfold.

25

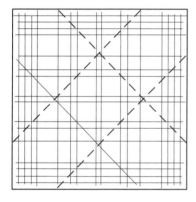

Repeat step 24
three more times.

26

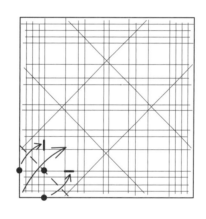

27

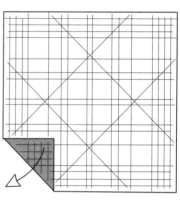

Unfold.

28

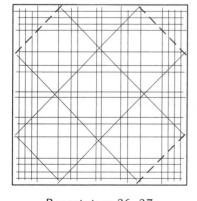

Repeat steps 26–27
three more times.

29

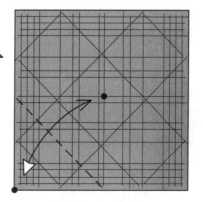

Fold and unfold.

30

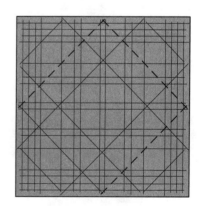

Repeat step 29
three more times.

31

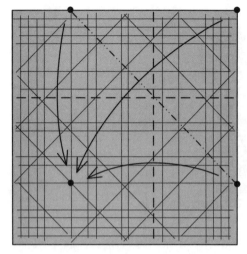

Fold along the creases. This
is similar to a preliminary
fold. The dots will meet.

32

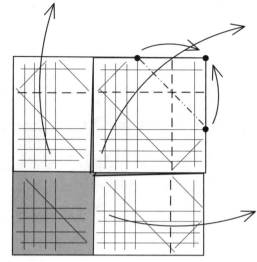

Fold along the creases.

33

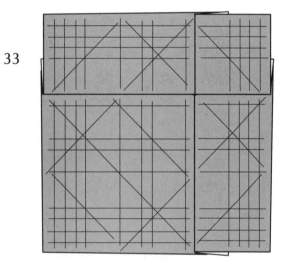

Repeat steps 31–32 going around.
You will have to be creative.

34

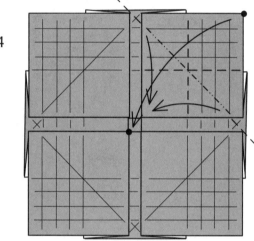

Fold along the creases.

35

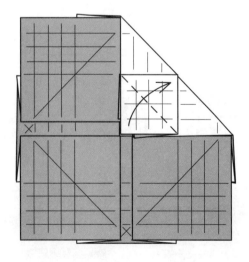

36

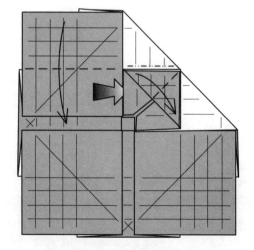

Squash-fold.

37

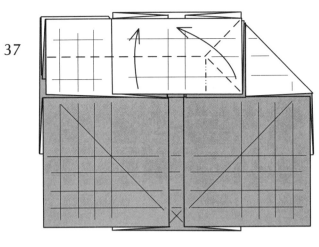

Squash-fold.

38

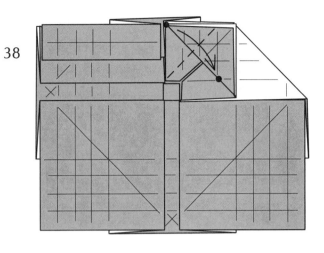

39

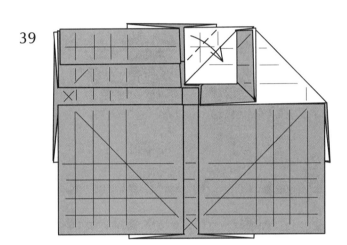

40

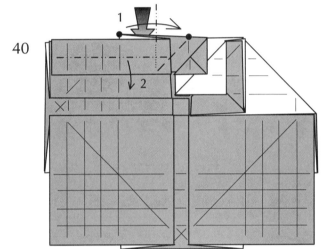

1. Squash fold so the dots meet.
2. This will happen automatically.

41

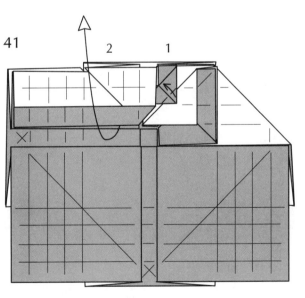

1. Fold up.
2. Unlock to fold up.

42

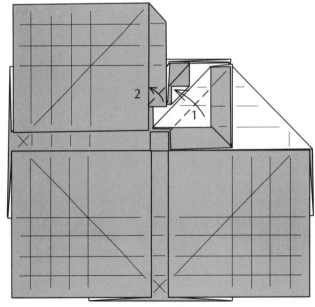

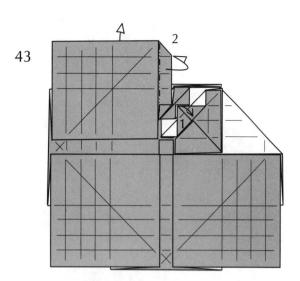

43

1. Fold down.
2. Fold behind along the mountain line while unfolding at the top.

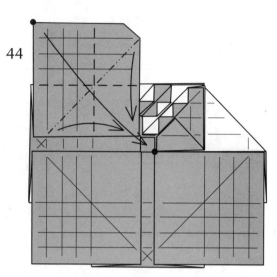

44

Fold along the creases.
The dots will meet.

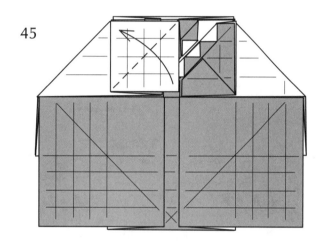

45

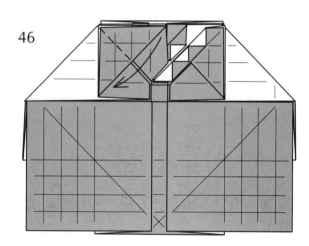

46

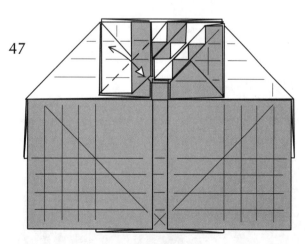

47

Fold and unfold.

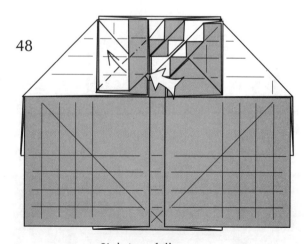

48

Sink (carefully so as not to rip the paper).

49

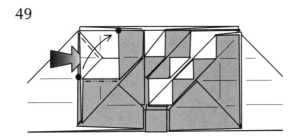

Only part of the model
is drawn. Squash-fold.

50

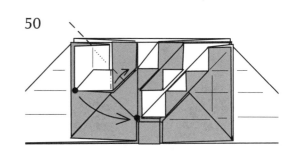

51

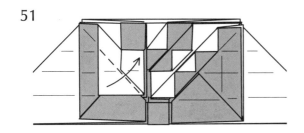

52

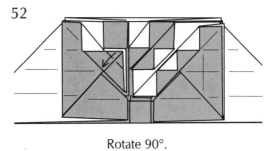

Rotate 90°.

53

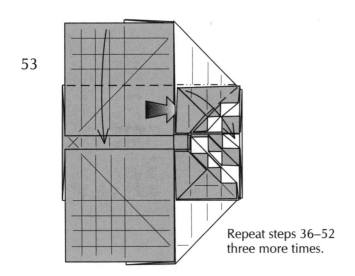

Repeat steps 36–52
three more times.

54

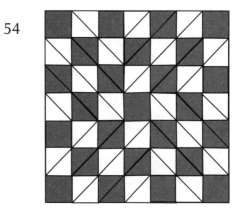

7 × 7 Chess Board

55

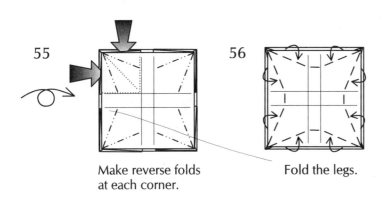

Make reverse folds
at each corner.

56

Fold the legs.

57

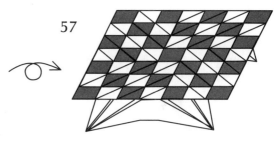

7 × 7 Chess Table

8 × 8 Chess Board & Table

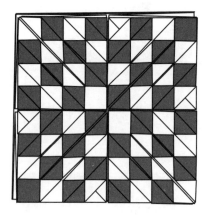

The length of the side of this chess board is 2/9 (or ≈ 0.222) that of the original square.

Stage 1: Precreasing.

1

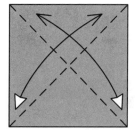

Fold and unfold.

2

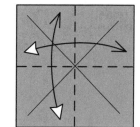

Fold and unfold.

3

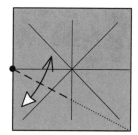

Fold and unfold on the left. Rotate 90°.

4

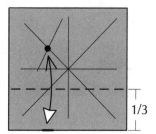

1/3

Fold and unfold.

5

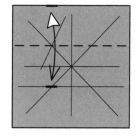

Fold and unfold.

6

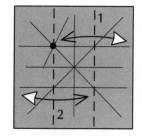

1

2

Fold and unfold.

7

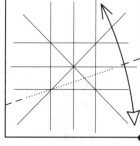

Fold and unfold on the left and right.

8

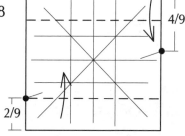

4/9

2/9

9

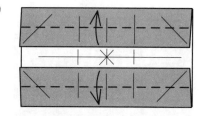

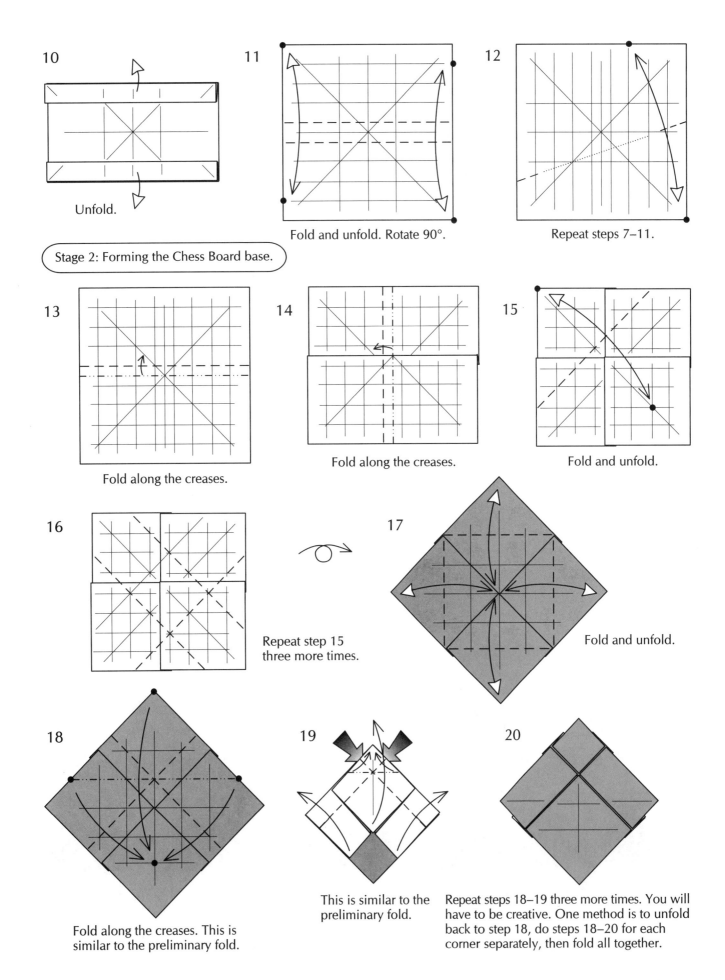

10

Unfold.

11

Fold and unfold. Rotate 90°.

12

Repeat steps 7–11.

Stage 2: Forming the Chess Board base.

13

Fold along the creases.

14

Fold along the creases.

15

Fold and unfold.

16

Repeat step 15 three more times.

17

Fold and unfold.

18

Fold along the creases. This is similar to the preliminary fold.

19

This is similar to the preliminary fold.

20

Repeat steps 18–19 three more times. You will have to be creative. One method is to unfold back to step 18, do steps 18–20 for each corner separately, then fold all together.

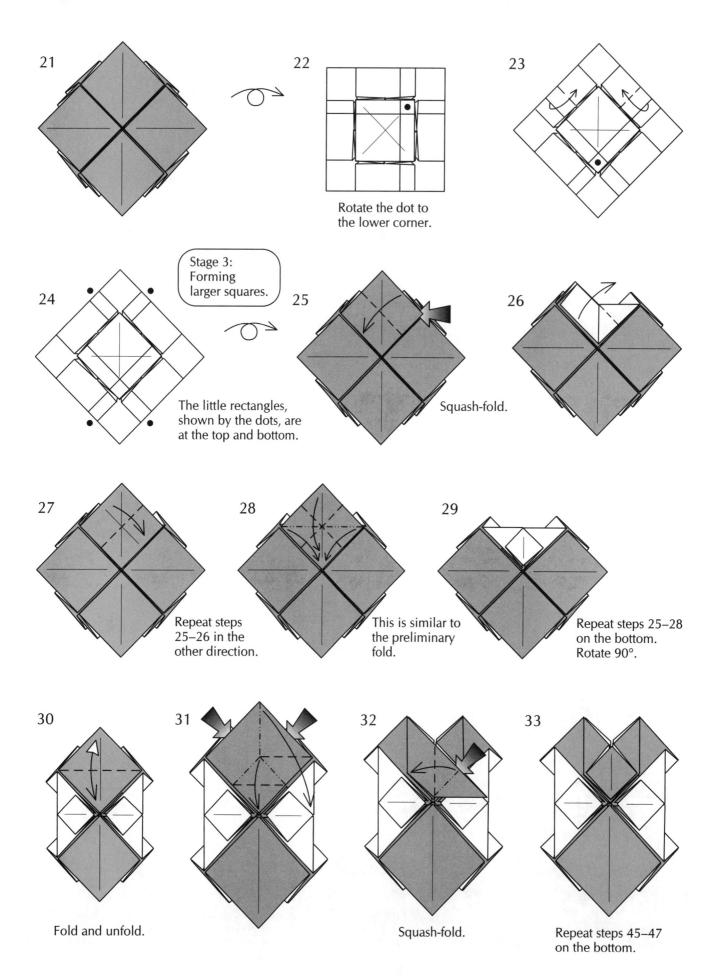

21

22 Rotate the dot to the lower corner.

23

Stage 3: Forming larger squares.

24 The little rectangles, shown by the dots, are at the top and bottom.

25 Squash-fold.

26

27 Repeat steps 25–26 in the other direction.

28 This is similar to the preliminary fold.

29 Repeat steps 25–28 on the bottom. Rotate 90°.

30 Fold and unfold.

31

32 Squash-fold.

33 Repeat steps 45–47 on the bottom.

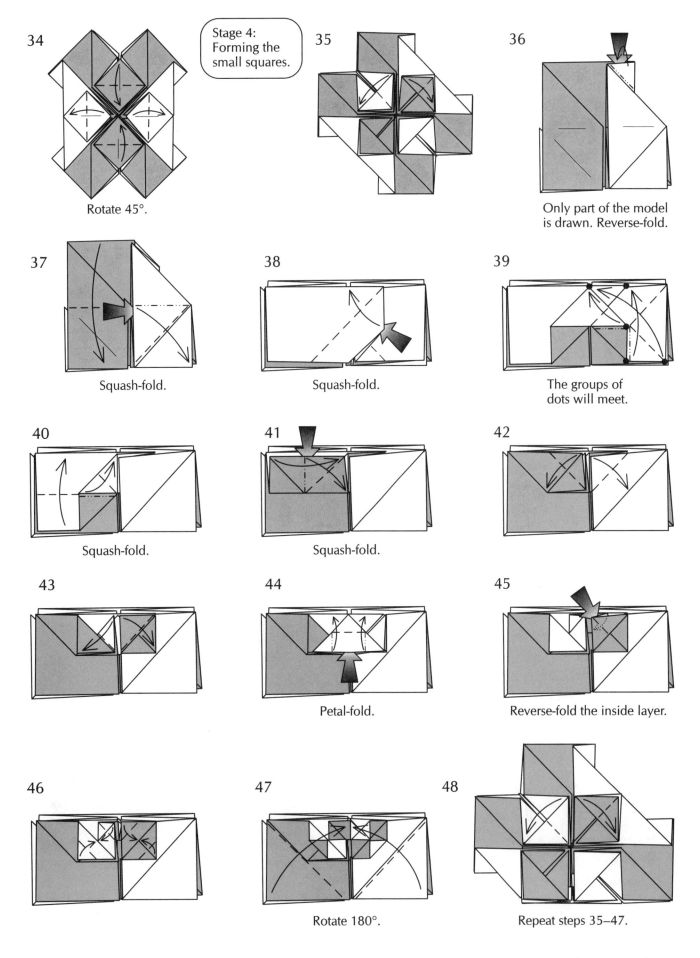

34

Rotate 45°.

Stage 4:
Forming the
small squares.

35

36

Only part of the model
is drawn. Reverse-fold.

37

Squash-fold.

38

Squash-fold.

39

The groups of
dots will meet.

40

Squash-fold.

41

Squash-fold.

42

43

44

Petal-fold.

45

Reverse-fold the inside layer.

46

47

Rotate 180°.

48

Repeat steps 35–47.

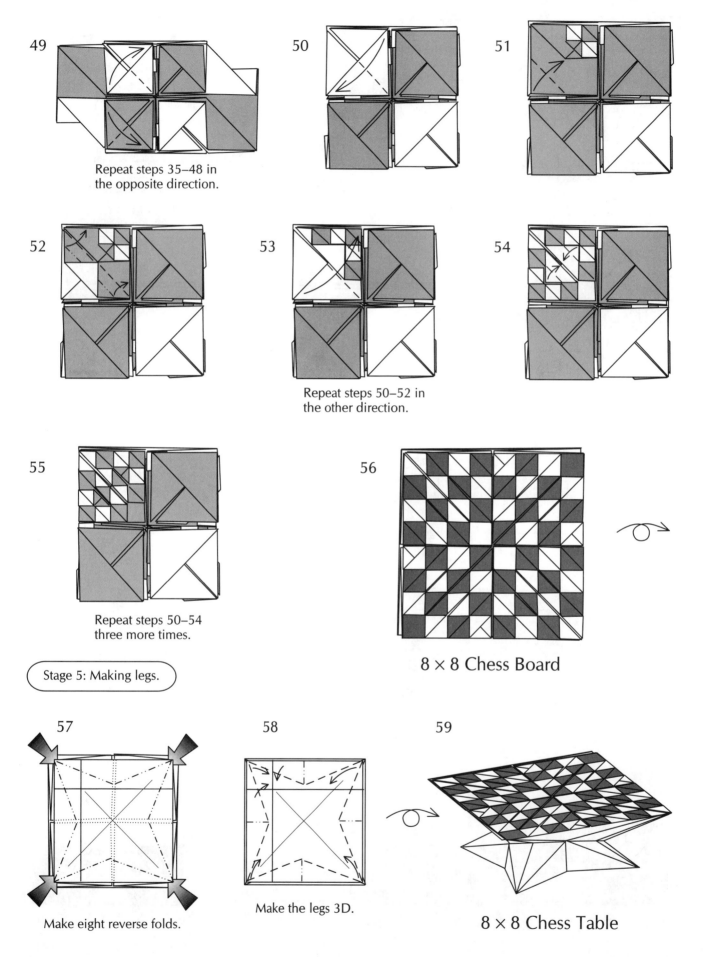

49

Repeat steps 35–48 in
the opposite direction.

50

51

52

53

Repeat steps 50–52 in
the other direction.

54

55

Repeat steps 50–54
three more times.

Stage 5: Making legs.

56

8 × 8 Chess Board

57

Make eight reverse folds.

58

Make the legs 3D.

59

8 × 8 Chess Table

Five Sides of Origami

Five-Pointed Star

Puffy Five-Pointed Star

Puffy Diamond Star

Five sided origami models are stunning. To create them from square paper often requires math. For models incorporating the pentagon, angles of 9°, 18°, and 36° are used. I show methods to find these easily and exactly.

The five-sided square is introduced and used for two flowers.

For another example of five-sided origami, also see the pentagon from the Polygon section.

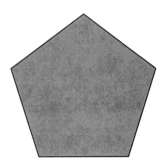

Pentagon

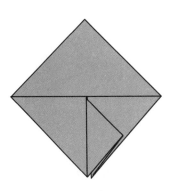

Five-Sided Square

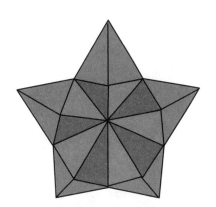

Five-Pointed Flower

Lily

Pentagonal Angles

These angles are exact and the folding methods were found from my procedure,
On the Edge (page 116). Some of these folding methods are used in several models
including the pentagon, golden rectangle, and others from this section.

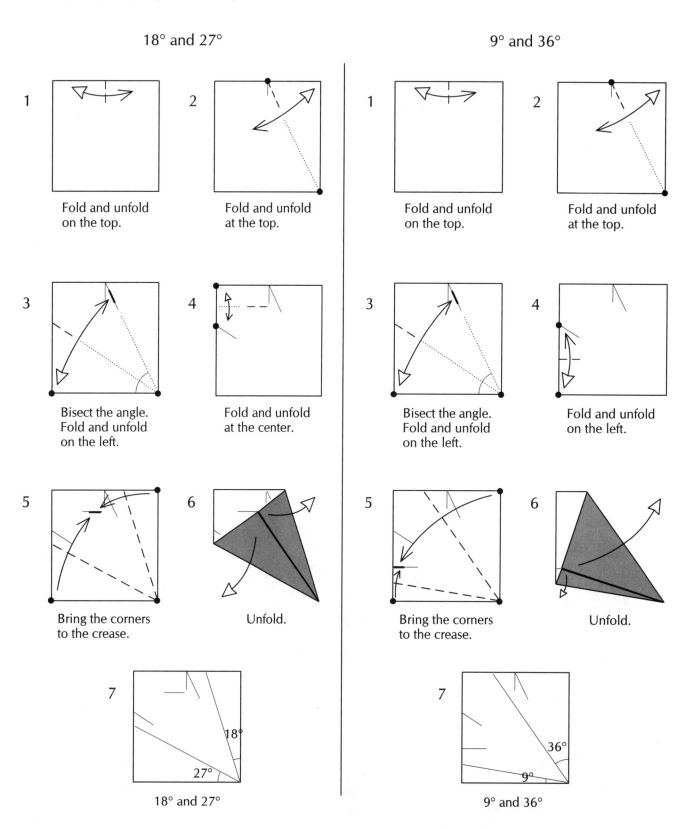

18° and 27°

1 Fold and unfold on the top.

2 Fold and unfold at the top.

3 Bisect the angle. Fold and unfold on the left.

4 Fold and unfold at the center.

5 Bring the corners to the crease.

6 Unfold.

7 18° and 27°

9° and 36°

1 Fold and unfold on the top.

2 Fold and unfold at the top.

3 Bisect the angle. Fold and unfold on the left.

4 Fold and unfold on the left.

5 Bring the corners to the crease.

6 Unfold.

7 9° and 36°

Five-Pointed Star

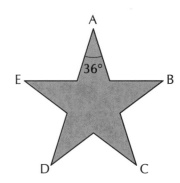

The five-pointed star is a beautiful shape. Each point has an angle of 36°. For a convenient crease pattern, let the top point come from the center of the square paper, and the four other points come from the corners of the square.

Math

The crease pattern shows the location of the five points (A, B, C, D, and E). Two landmarks, p and q are used.

Landmark p is 9° from the bottom.

Landmark q is used to fold along a line so point E is correctly placed. (The x-ray line is used in the calculation of q.) A difficult calculation shows

$q \approx .19958$

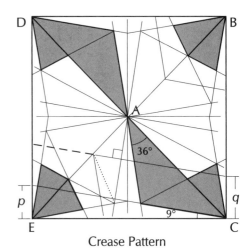

Crease Pattern

A quick method to approximate q is by folding an 11.25° line.

$q \approx \tan(11.25°) = \tan(45°/4) \approx .19891$

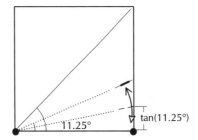

Folding Directions

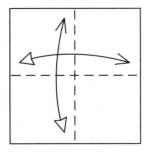

Fold and unfold.

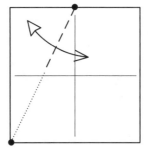

Fold and unfold creasing lightly on the top half.

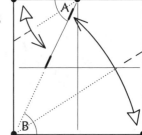

Fold and unfold on the edges to bisect the angles A and B.

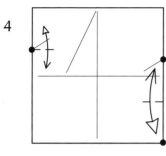

4 Fold and unfold on the edges.

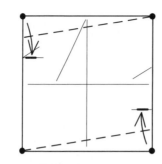

5 Bring the corners to the creases.

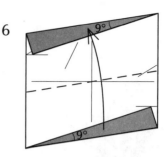

6 The two angles at the top and bottom are exactly 9°, each folded by a different method. Bring the edges together.

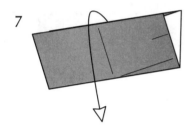

7 Unfold everything.

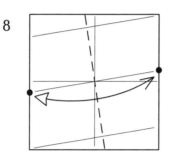

8 Fold and unfold.

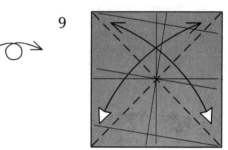

9 Fold and unfold.

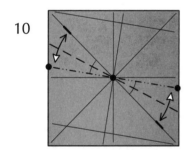

10 Fold and unfold to bisect the angles. Mountain-fold along the creases and push in at the center dot.

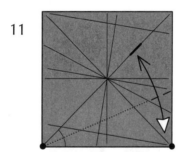

11 Bring the edge to the diagonal. Fold and unfold on the right.

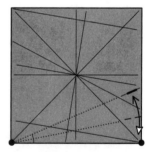

12 Fold and unfold on the right to bisect the angle.

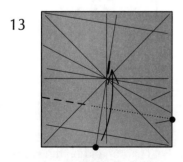

13 Fold on the left.

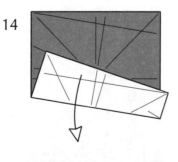

14 Unfold and rotate 180°.

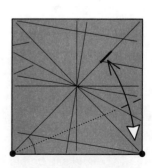

15 Repeat steps 11–14.

16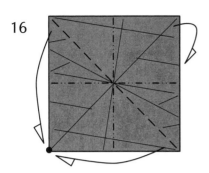

Make the preliminary fold and rotate so the dot is at the bottom.

17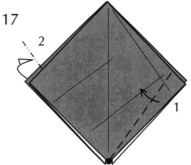

1. Fold along a hidden crease.
2. Turn over and repeat.

18

1. Fold along the hidden edge.
2. Turn over and repeat.

19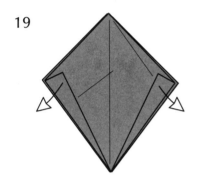

Unfold and repeat behind.

20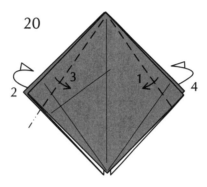

1 and 2. Fold along the creases.
3 and 4. Fold to match.

21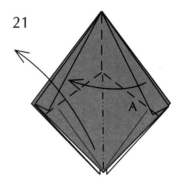

Fold the bottom up and to the left along the creases. There is no crease at A, but fold to match. Turn over and repeat.

22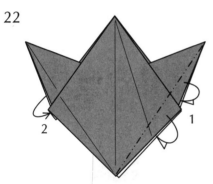

1. Fold behind along the creases on the right.
2. Turn over and repeat.

23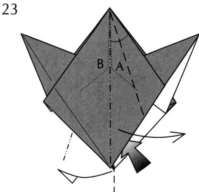

Begin by folding the bottom, top layer, to the right. Turn over and repeat. Only fold along the creases. A and B are hidden white layers, A will slide above B.

24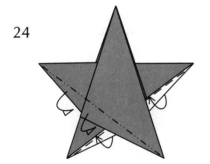

Tuck inside along the creases. Turn over and repeat.

25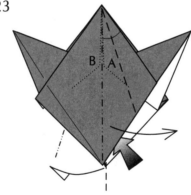

Five-Pointed Star

Puffy Five-Pointed Star

The traditional puffy star comes from a strip of paper, folded into a knot to make a pentagon. The rest of the strip wraps around the pentagon, and the model is puffed out. Here is my version from a square sheet.

Math

The layout is composed of two adjacent pentagons. It is placed on a square sheet with horizontal edges for the top and bottom to allow for tabs. To ease the math and folding, the height of each pentagon is set at .5.

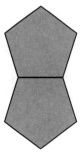

Layout

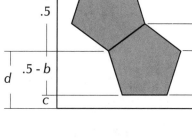

Crease Pattern

Landmarks will be found.

Let a = length of sides of pentagon
b = height of top of pentagon
c = height of tab
d = height from bottom of square to where the pentagons meet
e = landmark to divide the square with a 36° line going through the center.

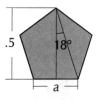

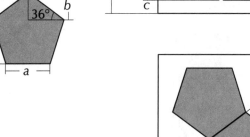

$a = \tan(18°)$
$b = a * \sin(36°)$
$c = b/2$
$d = (1 - b)/2$
$e = (1 - \tan(36°))/2$

The landmarks are:

$c \approx .09549$
$d \approx .40451$
$e \approx .13673$

Landmarks c, d, and e are found easily and exactly. A few folds find c (at 4) and d (at 5).

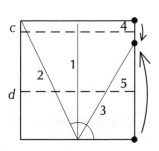

Landmark e is found by folding 36°.

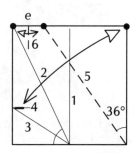

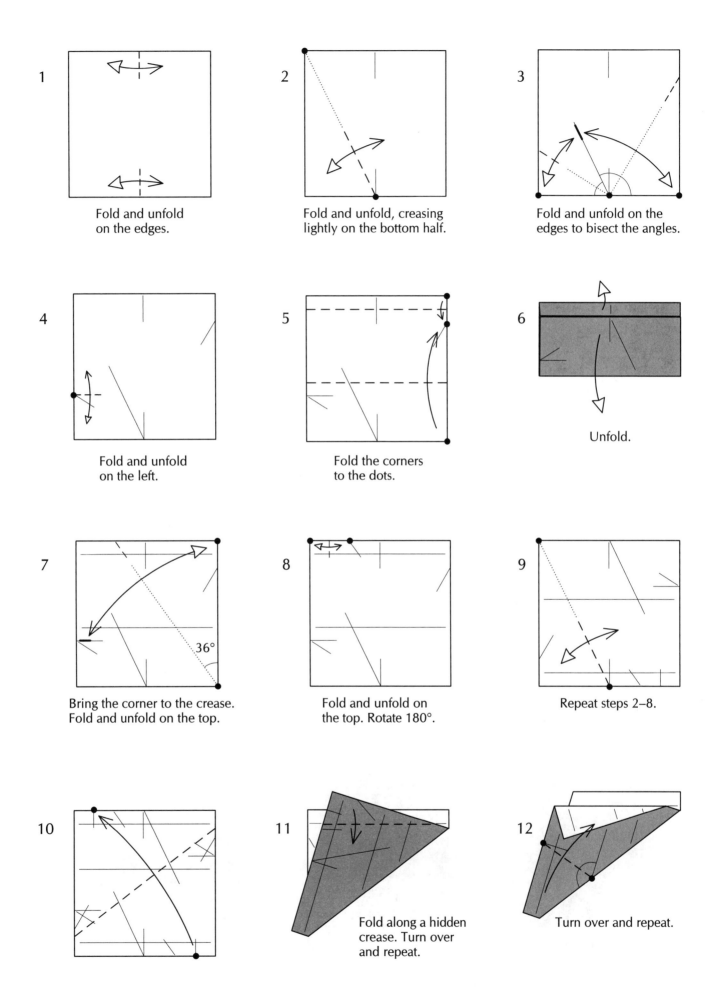

1 Fold and unfold on the edges.

2 Fold and unfold, creasing lightly on the bottom half.

3 Fold and unfold on the edges to bisect the angles.

4 Fold and unfold on the left.

5 Fold the corners to the dots.

6 Unfold.

7 Bring the corner to the crease. Fold and unfold on the top.

36°

8 Fold and unfold on the top. Rotate 180°.

9 Repeat steps 2–8.

10

11 Fold along a hidden crease. Turn over and repeat.

12 Turn over and repeat.

Puffy Five-Pointed Star 75

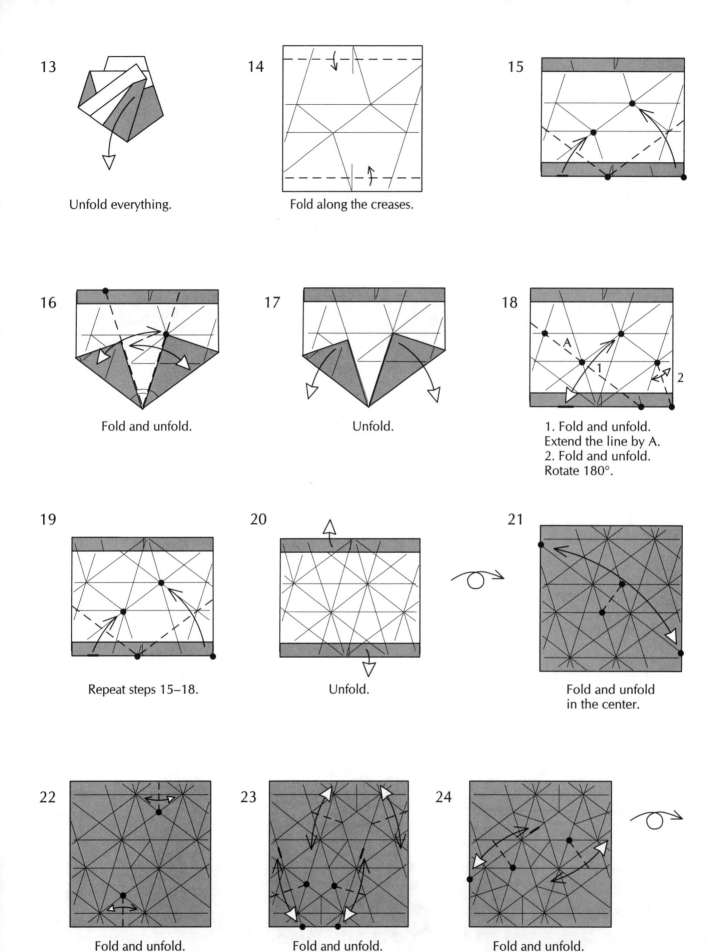

13   Unfold everything.

14   Fold along the creases.

15

16   Fold and unfold.

17   Unfold.

18   1. Fold and unfold.
Extend the line by A.
2. Fold and unfold.
Rotate 180°.

19   Repeat steps 15–18.

20   Unfold.

21   Fold and unfold
in the center.

22   Fold and unfold.

23   Fold and unfold.

24   Fold and unfold.

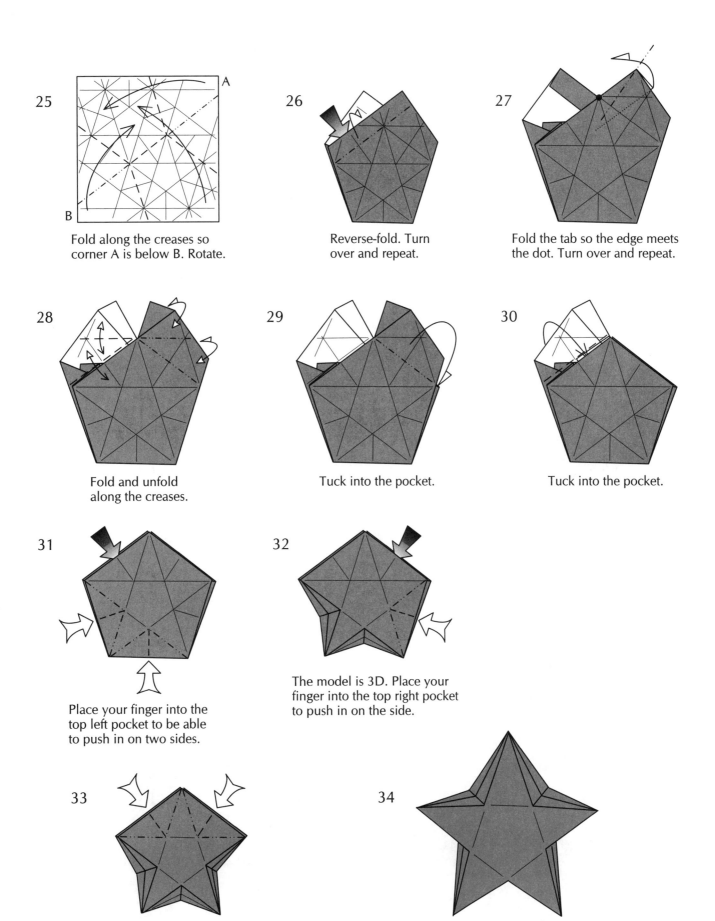

25 Fold along the creases so corner A is below B. Rotate.

26 Reverse-fold. Turn over and repeat.

27 Fold the tab so the edge meets the dot. Turn over and repeat.

28 Fold and unfold along the creases.

29 Tuck into the pocket.

30 Tuck into the pocket.

31 Place your finger into the top left pocket to be able to push in on two sides.

32 The model is 3D. Place your finger into the top right pocket to push in on the side.

33 Push in on two more sides.

34

Puffy Five-Pointed Star

Puffy Diamond Star

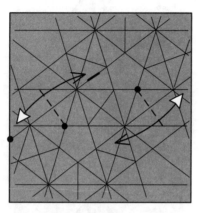

1

This is a variation of the Puffy Five-Pointed Star. The model radiates from the bottom point.

This is step 24 of the Puffy Five-Pointed Star. Fold and unfold.

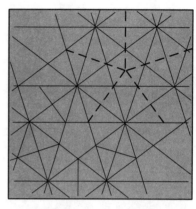

2

Fold and unfold along the creases and extend them to their center.

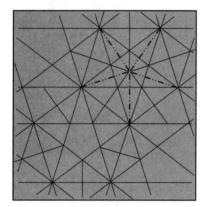

3

Fold and unfold new creases that meet at their center.

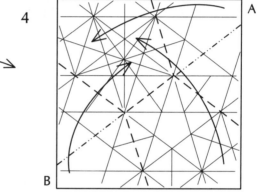

4

Continue with steps 25–30 of the Puffy Five-Pointed Star.

A

B

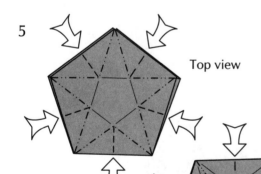

5

Top view

Bottom view

Push in on the sides. At the bottom, puff out at the dot and push in on the sides.

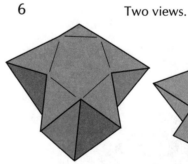

6

Two views.

Puffy Diamond Star

Five-Sided Square

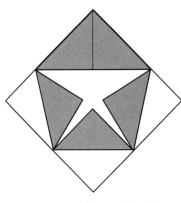

The Five-Sided Square is an interesting base. This base is composed of five triangular sides that flatten into a square with one hidden side. Several models from a square can be folded from this base to gain a fifth side. Two examples using traditional models are given. The fortune teller from the blintz base, and lily from the frog base, are folded from the Five-Sided Square to create flowers with five petals.

Math

Calculate the landmarks.

> The largest pentagon is placed in the square so all the sides, A, are congruent. However, this is not the uniform pentagon (the top angle is 90°). Find landmarks A, B, C, D. Only one is required since all the others can be folded from it.

$$A + B = C + D = 1$$
$$B^2 + C^2 = A^2$$
$$A = \sqrt{2}D \quad \text{since } D^2 + D^2 = A^2$$

The solution to these four equations with four unknowns is:

$$A = 2 + \sqrt{2} - \sqrt{4\sqrt{2} + 2} \approx .64711$$

$$B = -1 - \sqrt{2} + \sqrt{4\sqrt{2} + 2} \approx .35289$$

$$C = -\sqrt{2} + \sqrt{2\sqrt{2} + 1} \approx .54242$$

$$D = \sqrt{2} + 1 - \sqrt{2\sqrt{2} + 1} \approx .45758$$

A folding sequence for landmark D is found from my procedure, On the Edge (page 116).

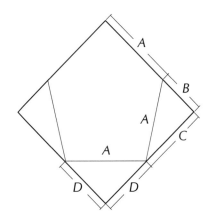

Crease pattern of Five-Sided Square

Folding Directions

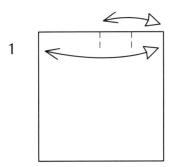

1 Fold and unfold on the top to find the quarter mark.

2 Bring the bottom right corner to the left edge. Crease on the bottom. Landmark D is found.

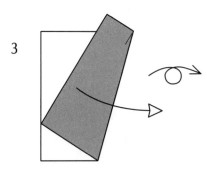

3 Unfold.

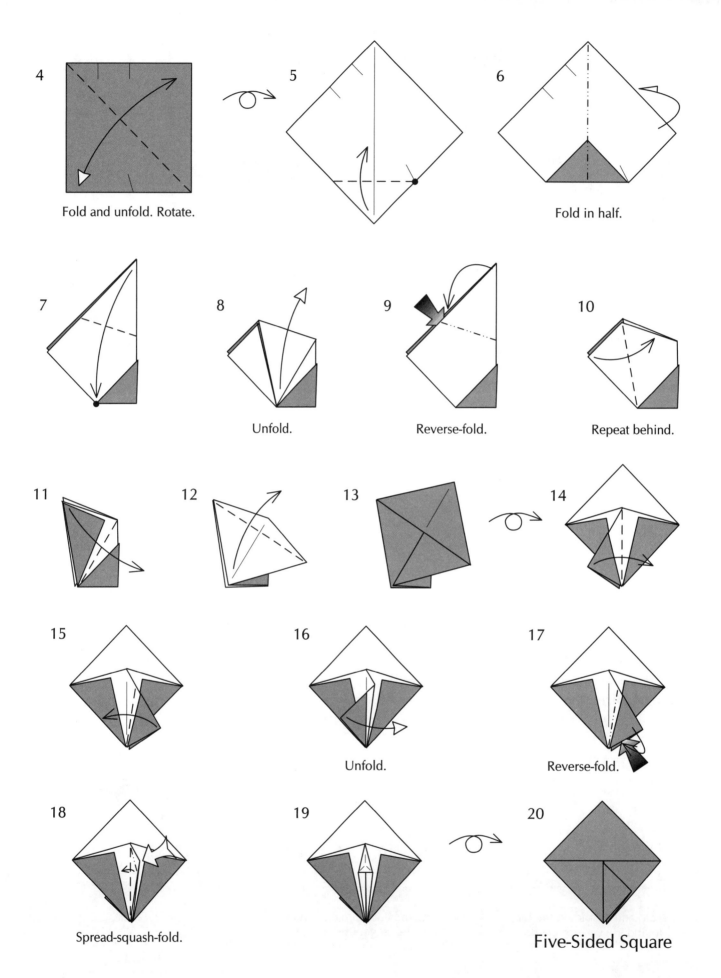

4 Fold and unfold. Rotate.

5

6 Fold in half.

7

8 Unfold.

9 Reverse-fold.

10 Repeat behind.

11

12

13

14

15

16 Unfold.

17 Reverse-fold.

18 Spread-squash-fold.

19

20 Five-Sided Square

Five-Pointed Flower

The five-sided square is applied to the traditional fortune teller. The four sides of the fortune teller become a beautiful three dimensional five-pointed flower.

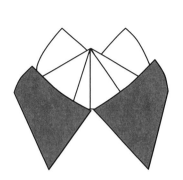

Traditional Fortune Teller

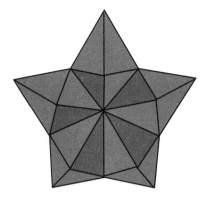

Five-Pointed Flower

1

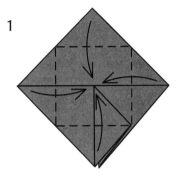

Begin with the Five-Sided Square. Fold four corners to the center.

2

3

4

5

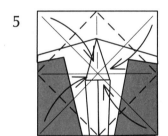

Fold four corners to the center.

6

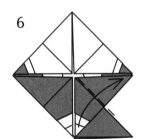

7

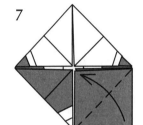

8

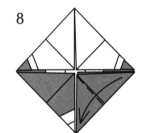

9

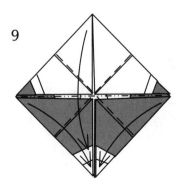

This is similar to the preliminary fold.

10

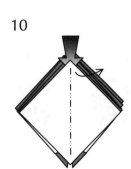

Spread all around.

11

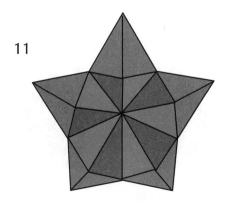

Five-Pointed Flower

Lily

This lily is a variation of the traditional lily from the frog base. By using the Five-Sided Square, the preliminary fold is formed with an extra side.

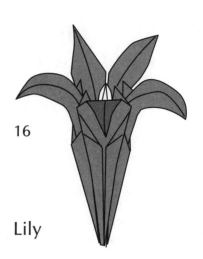

16

Lily

1

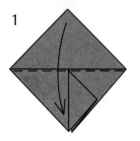

Begin with the
Five-Sided Square.

2

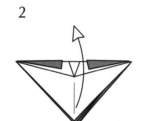

Unfold.

3 4

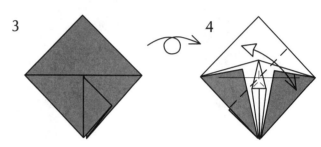

Fold and unfold.

5

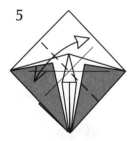

Fold and unfold.

6

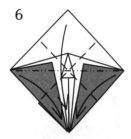

This is similar to the
preliminary fold.

7

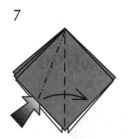

Squash-fold.

8

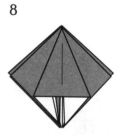

Squash-fold
all the sides.

9

Fold inside.

10

Fold inside on
all the sides.

11 12

Thin.

13

Thin on all
the sides.

14

Rotate 180°.

15

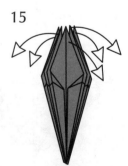

Curl the petals.

Structure & Proportion

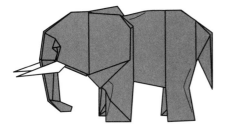  

Designing and folding animals is a wonderful and challenging experience. A wide variety of animals and other subjects can be created through the concept of Structure and Proportion. It gives the designer control to find good shapes efficiently.

A structure is a family of related bases. The proportion refers to the overall shape of the animal, or a particular base used to yield the correct proportions.

The principles of Structure and Proportion help meet the following ideals that I have for designing animals:
1. The model is not too difficult.
2. The paper is used efficiently to make an animal as large as possible.
3. The model can be folded from standard origami paper (kami).
4. It stays in shape without spreading.
5. The animal is appealing with good proportions and detail.
6. The animal has clean lines and a seamless closed back if possible.
7. A variety of related animals can be folded by related methods.
8. Understand that origami is an experience for the folder as much as it is a visual art.

Example of Structure & Proportion

Take a look at the following base.

1

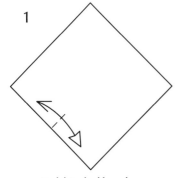

Fold in half and
unfold on the left.

2

Fold and unfold.

3

1. Fold up.
2. Fold to make a right
angle at the dot.

4

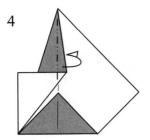

Fold behind along the hidden crease.
Repeat steps 3–4 on the right.

5

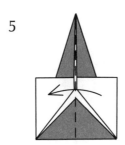

Fold in half
and rotate.

6

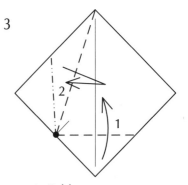

Here is a structure that can be used
as a base for many animals.

In the first step, the 1/2 mark was found on the edge. Compare what happens to the base if a different landmark is used in step 1.

Step 1:

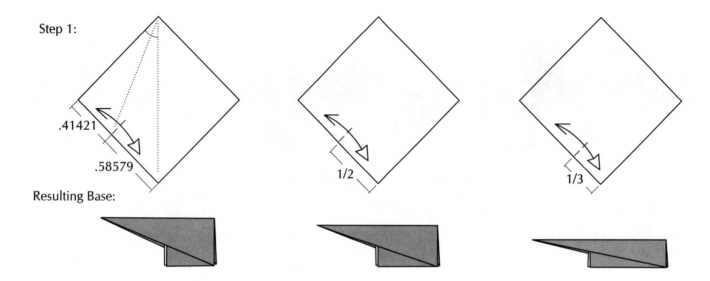

Resulting Base:

If the landmark of step 1 is smaller (closer to the bottom of the square), the resulting base is longer. This shows how one structure can yield many proportions. The proportions of the base are not the same as that of the animal to be folded from it, but it does determine it.

Proportion Formula for this Base

Given a from step 1, b is the length of the dotted line and c is the length as shown.

Let the proportion $P = b/c$ be that of the resulting base.

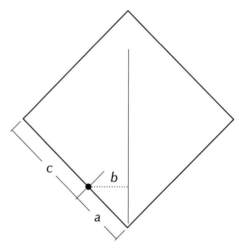

Landmark a sets up the proportion.

Given a, find P.

$$b = a/\sqrt{2}$$
$$c = 1 - a$$

$$P = b/c = a/(\sqrt{2}(1 - a))$$

Given P, find a:

From the previous equation, solving for a yields:

$$a = (\sqrt{2}P)/(1 + \sqrt{2}P)$$

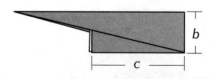

The proportion for this base is $P = b/c$.

Examples

Simple Elephant

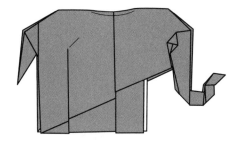

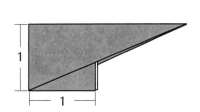

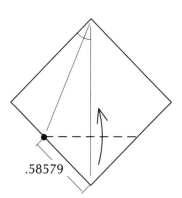

For this simple elephant, I chose to use the base where the width and height are the same, labeled as 1 for both. Thus $P = 1$.

Solving for a, $a = 2 - \sqrt{2} \approx .58579$

This simple landmark is found from the kite fold.

Dromedary

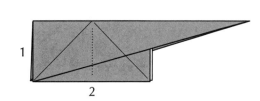

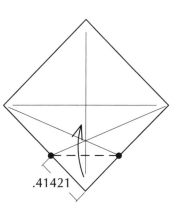

For the dromedary, the width is twice the height, so $P = .5$.

Solving for a, $a = \sqrt{2} - 1 \approx .41421$

This simple landmark is also found from the kite fold.

Camel

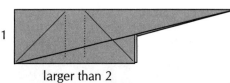

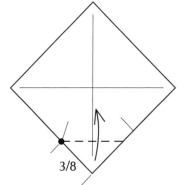

To use the method for the dromedary but allow for two humps, let the width be more than twice the height, so $P < .5$. Without actually solving any equation, but looking for an easy landmark, I chose $a = 3/8$. A calculation of P ($\approx .42426$) shows it to be fine.

Animal Proportions

To design an animal, it is important to consider the proportions.

For example, consider the elephant. If the body and legs were inscribed in a rectangle, would the rectangle be long, square, or tall?

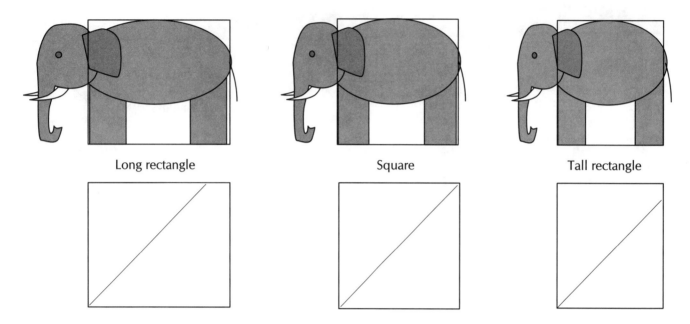

Long rectangle   Square   Tall rectangle

Answer: It would be inscribed in a tall rectangle.

A fun project for designing an animal is to make a trio to represent the subject as a (relatively) simple, intermediate, and complex work. All would have similar proportions but different structures to incorporate varying detail. I have created a trio of related elephants, simple, intermediate, and complex. All have similar proportions.

Design challenge: Choose a subject and create a trio of origami models with increasing number of details in each version.

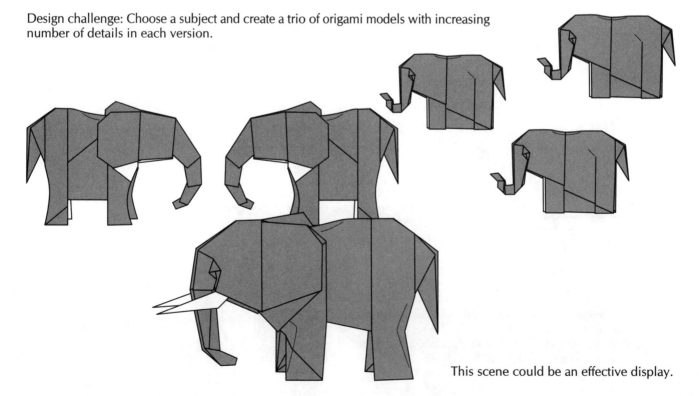

This scene could be an effective display.

Dromedary

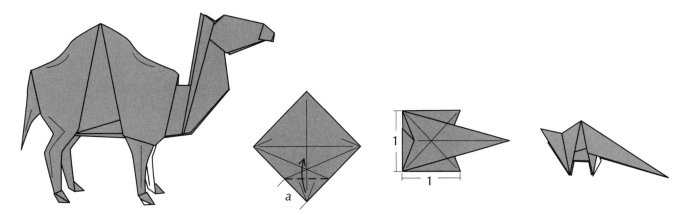

The dromedary uses the same structure as the camel and two of the elephants. Landmark a is different in each model for varying proportions. Here, $a = \sqrt{2} - 1 \approx .41421$ so the middle figure shows dimensions of 1×1, leading quickly to the shape in the third figure.

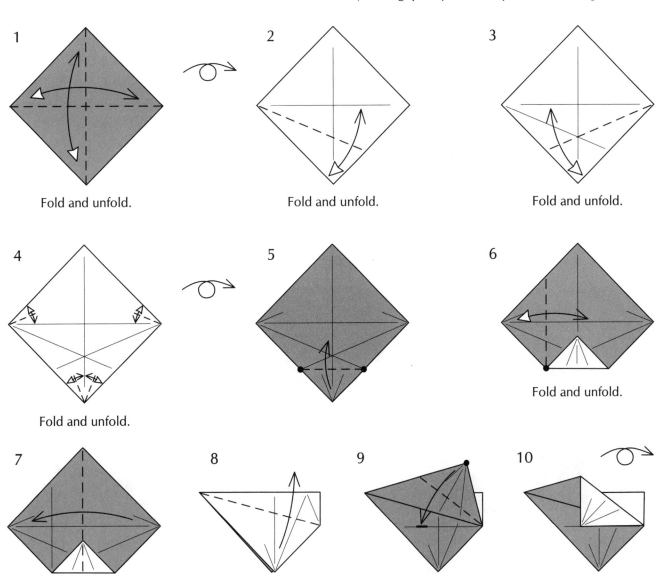

1

Fold and unfold.

2

Fold and unfold.

3

Fold and unfold.

4

Fold and unfold.

5

6

Fold and unfold.

7

Fold in half and rotate.

8

Fold the top layer.

9

10

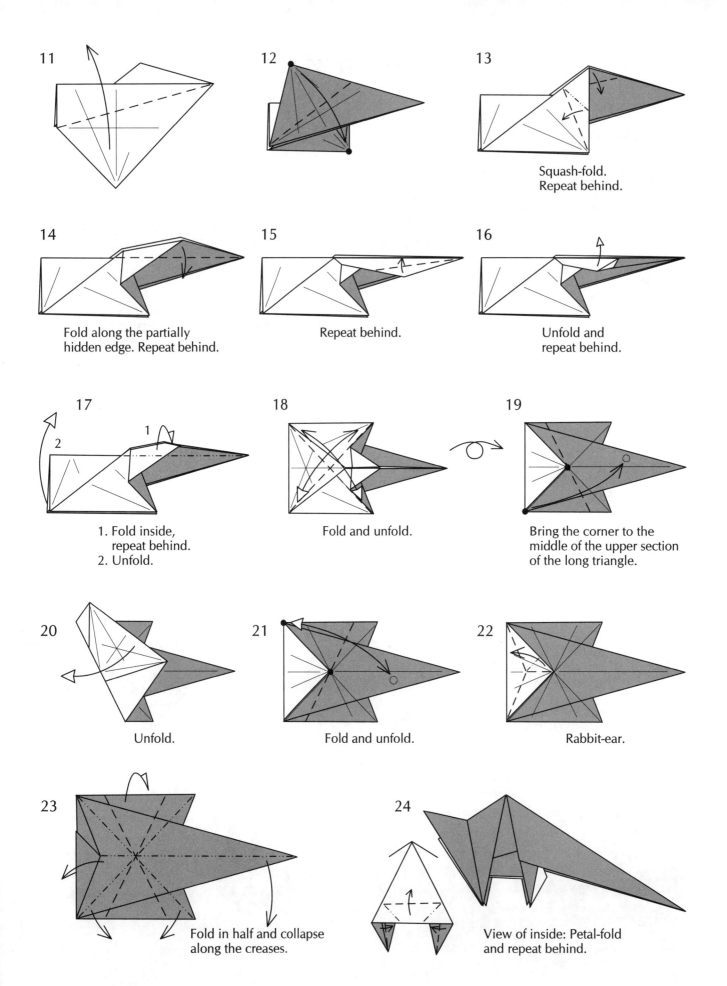

11

12

13

Squash-fold.
Repeat behind.

14

Fold along the partially
hidden edge. Repeat behind.

15

Repeat behind.

16

Unfold and
repeat behind.

17

1. Fold inside,
   repeat behind.
2. Unfold.

18

Fold and unfold.

19

Bring the corner to the
middle of the upper section
of the long triangle.

20

Unfold.

21

Fold and unfold.

22

Rabbit-ear.

23

Fold in half and collapse
along the creases.

24

View of inside: Petal-fold
and repeat behind.

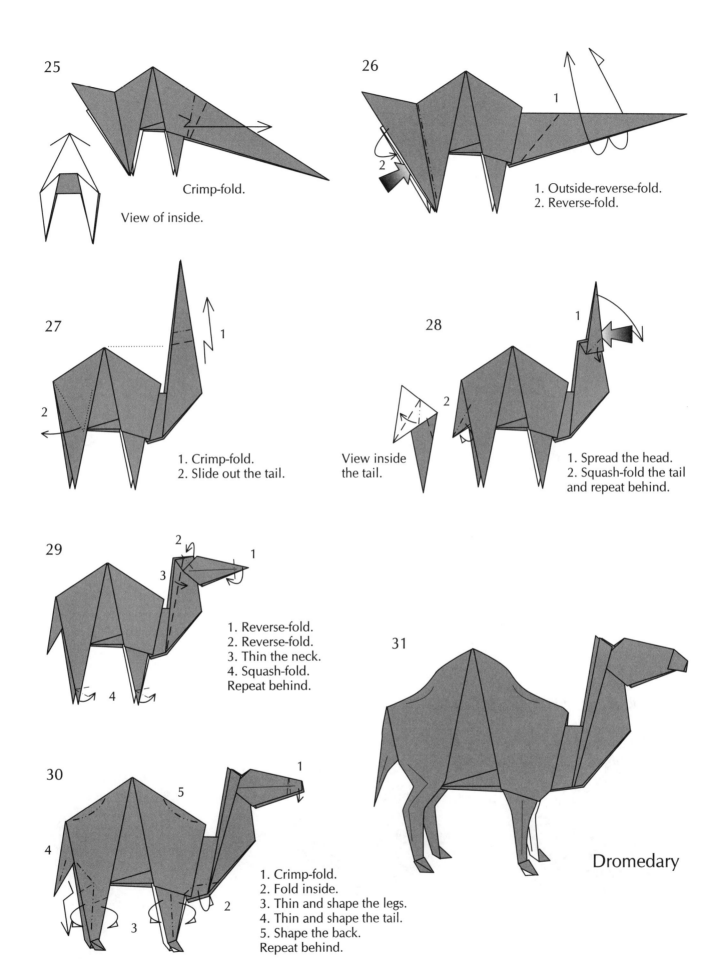

25

Crimp-fold.

View of inside.

26

1. Outside-reverse-fold.
2. Reverse-fold.

27

1. Crimp-fold.
2. Slide out the tail.

28

View inside
the tail.

1. Spread the head.
2. Squash-fold the tail
and repeat behind.

29

1. Reverse-fold.
2. Reverse-fold.
3. Thin the neck.
4. Squash-fold.
Repeat behind.

30

1. Crimp-fold.
2. Fold inside.
3. Thin and shape the legs.
4. Thin and shape the tail.
5. Shape the back.
Repeat behind.

31

Dromedary

Camel

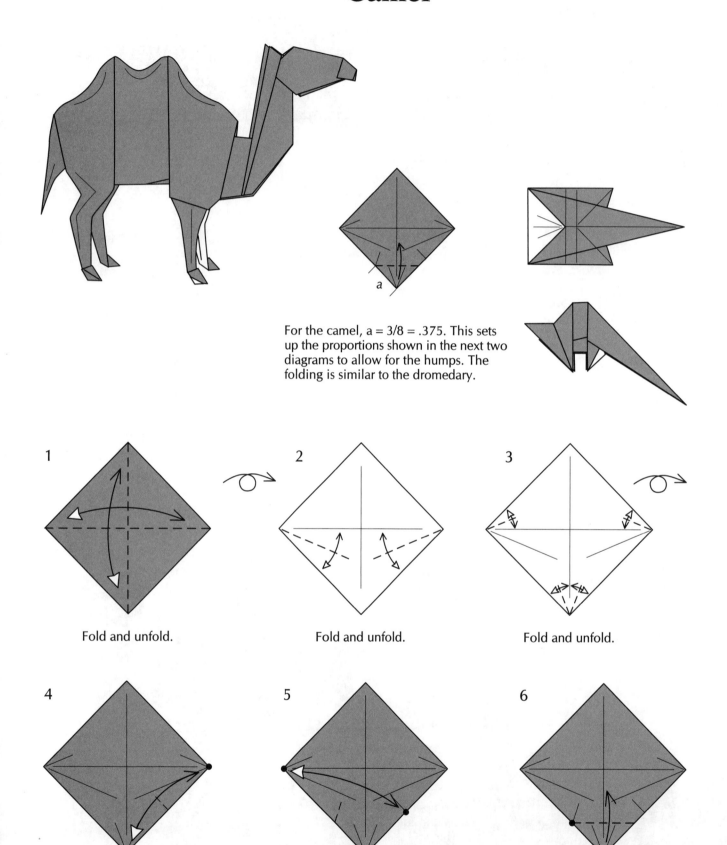

For the camel, a = 3/8 = .375. This sets up the proportions shown in the next two diagrams to allow for the humps. The folding is similar to the dromedary.

1

Fold and unfold.

2

Fold and unfold.

3

Fold and unfold.

4

Fold and unfold on the edge.

5

Fold and unfold on the edge.

6

7

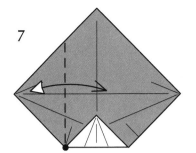

Fold and unfold.

8

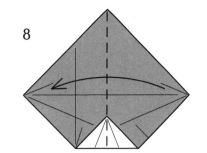

Fold in half and rotate.

9

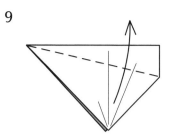

Fold the top layer.

10

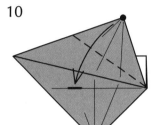

11

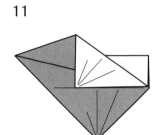

12

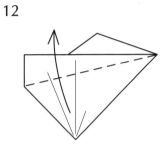

13

14

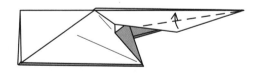

Squash-fold.
Repeat behind.

15

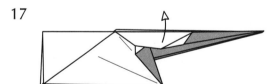

Fold along the partially
hidden edge. Repeat behind.

16

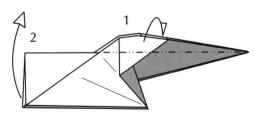

Repeat behind.

17

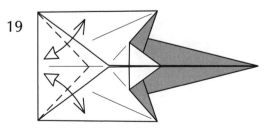

Unfold and repeat behind.

18

1. Fold inside, repeat behind.
2. Unfold.

19

Fold and unfold.

20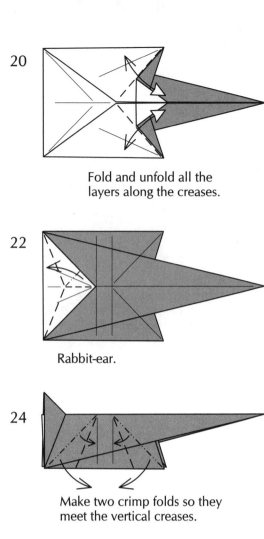

Fold and unfold all the
layers along the creases.

21

Fold and unfold.

22

Rabbit-ear.

23

Fold in half.

24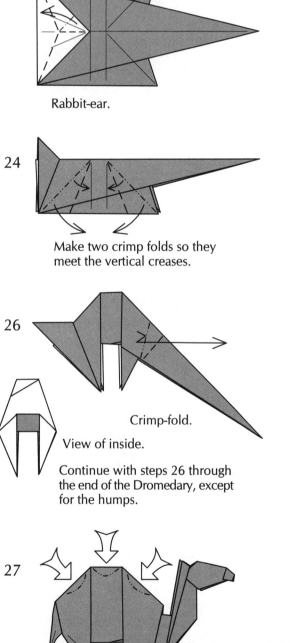

Make two crimp folds so they
meet the vertical creases.

25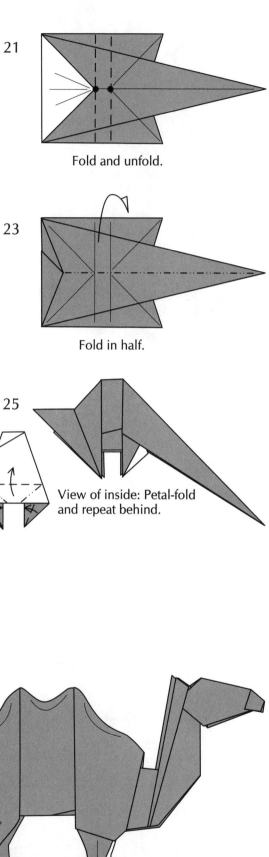

View of inside: Petal-fold
and repeat behind.

26

Crimp-fold.

View of inside.

Continue with steps 26 through
the end of the Dromedary, except
for the humps.

27

Shape the humps to
make the back 3D.

28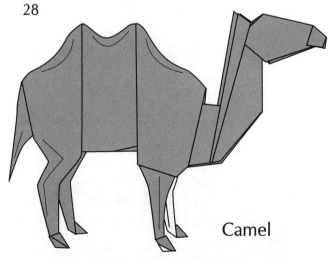

Camel

Llama

The llama is related to the camel and dromedary. The same neck and head folds are used. However, the body structure is different. This llama uses a structure similar to the rhinoceros but with different proportions. In step 9, the bottom corner is folded up with a landmark that sets up the proportions.

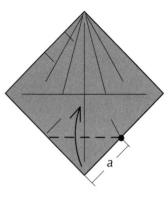

$a = .4571$

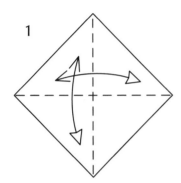

1

Fold and unfold.

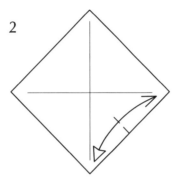

2

Fold and unfold on the bottom right.

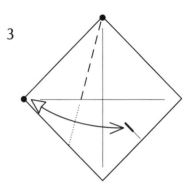

3

Bring the left corner to the crease. Fold and unfold on the top half.

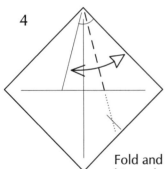

4

Fold and unfold to bisect the angle.

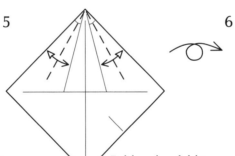

5

Fold and unfold to bisect the angles.

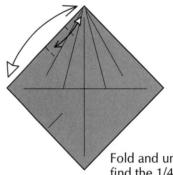

6

Fold and unfold to find the 1/4 mark.

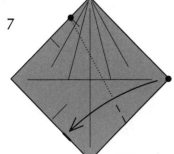

7

Using the 1/4 mark on the upper left, bring the right corner to the edge. Crease on the right.

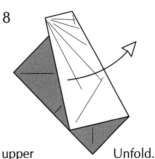

8

Unfold.

9

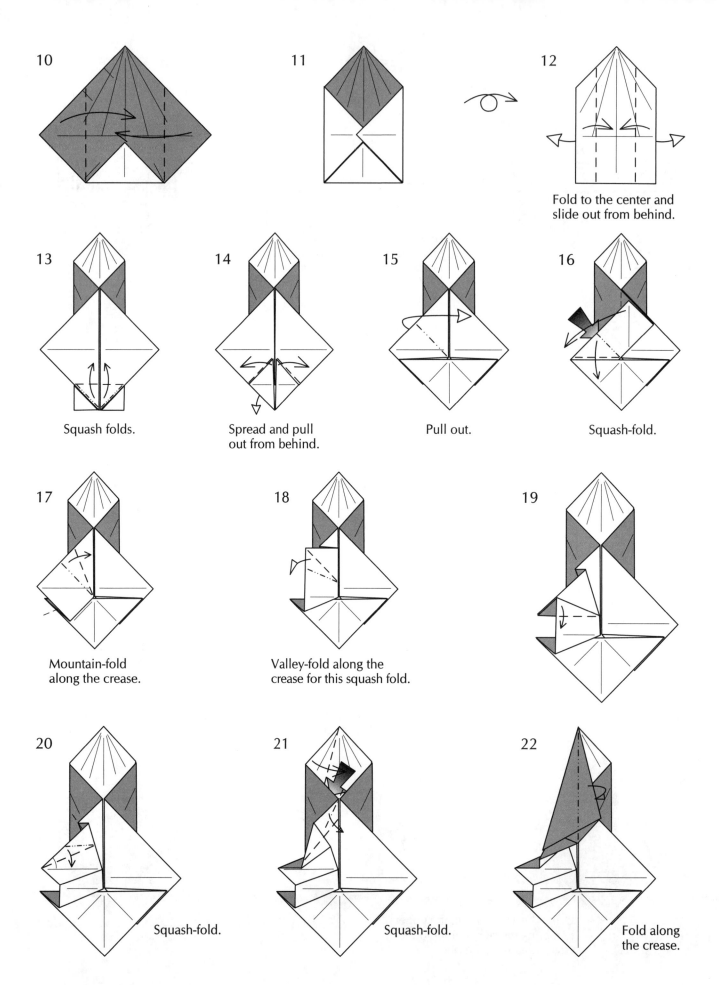

10

11

12

Fold to the center and
slide out from behind.

13

Squash folds.

14

Spread and pull
out from behind.

15

Pull out.

16

Squash-fold.

17

Mountain-fold
along the crease.

18

Valley-fold along the
crease for this squash fold.

19

20

Squash-fold.

21

Squash-fold.

22

Fold along
the crease.

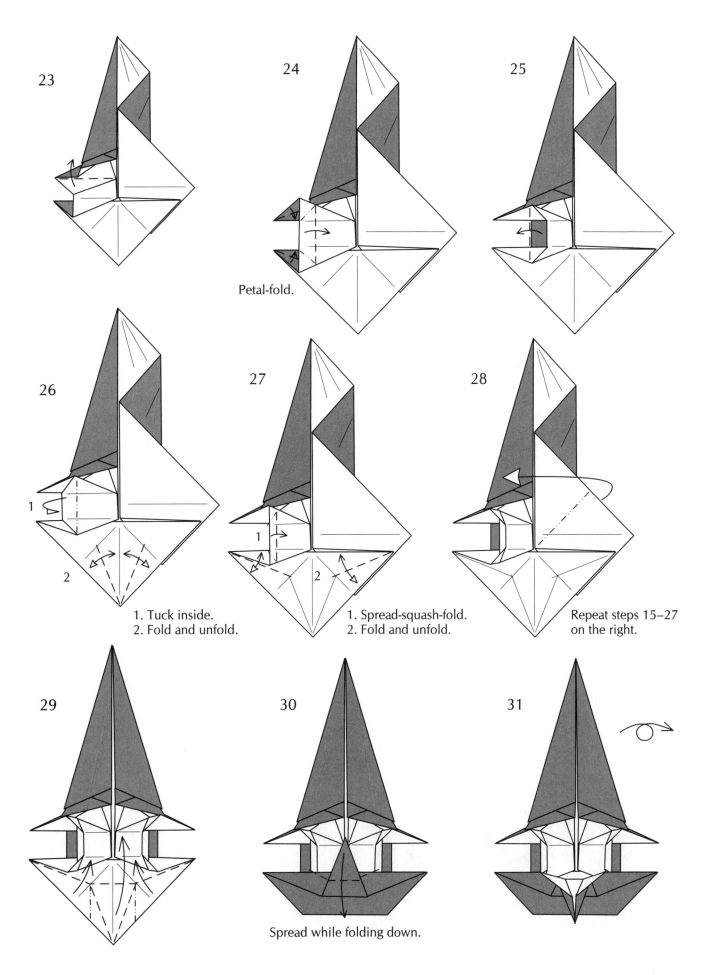

23

24

Petal-fold.

25

26

1. Tuck inside.
2. Fold and unfold.

27

1. Spread-squash-fold.
2. Fold and unfold.

28

Repeat steps 15–27
on the right.

29

30

Spread while folding down.

31

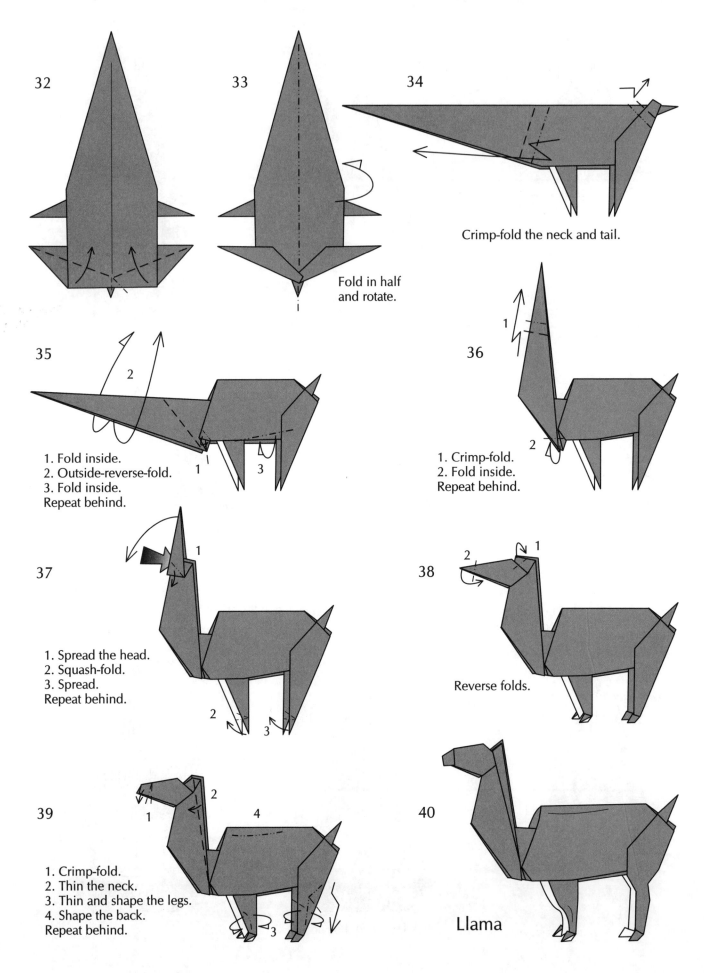

32

33

Fold in half
and rotate.

34

Crimp-fold the neck and tail.

35

2

1. Fold inside.
2. Outside-reverse-fold.
3. Fold inside.
Repeat behind.

1

3

36

1

2

1. Crimp-fold.
2. Fold inside.
Repeat behind.

37

1

1. Spread the head.
2. Squash-fold.
3. Spread.
Repeat behind.

2

3

38

2

1

Reverse folds.

39

1

2

4

1. Crimp-fold.
2. Thin the neck.
3. Thin and shape the legs.
4. Shape the back.
Repeat behind.

3

40

Llama

Rhinoceros

The rhinoceros uses a structure similar to the llama but with different proportions. The landmark found in step 4 is lower than that of the llama, to allow for a more squat animal.

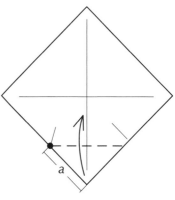

$$a = 1 - 1/\sqrt{3} \approx .4226$$

1

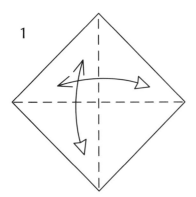

Fold and unfold.

2

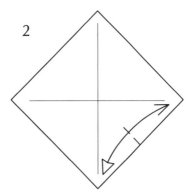

Fold and unfold on the bottom right.

3

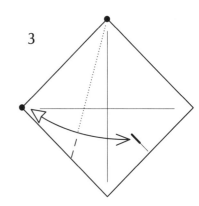

Bring the left corner to the crease. Fold and unfold on the bottom left.

4

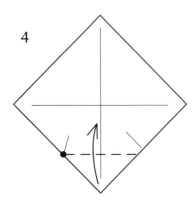

5

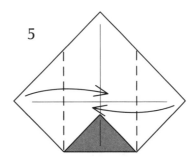

6

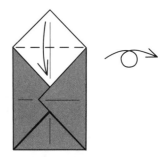

7

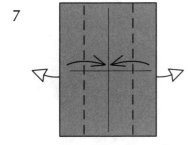

Fold to the center and slide out from behind.

8

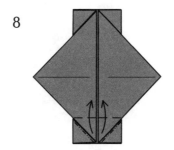

Squash folds.

9

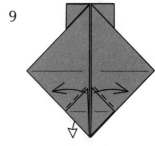

Spread.

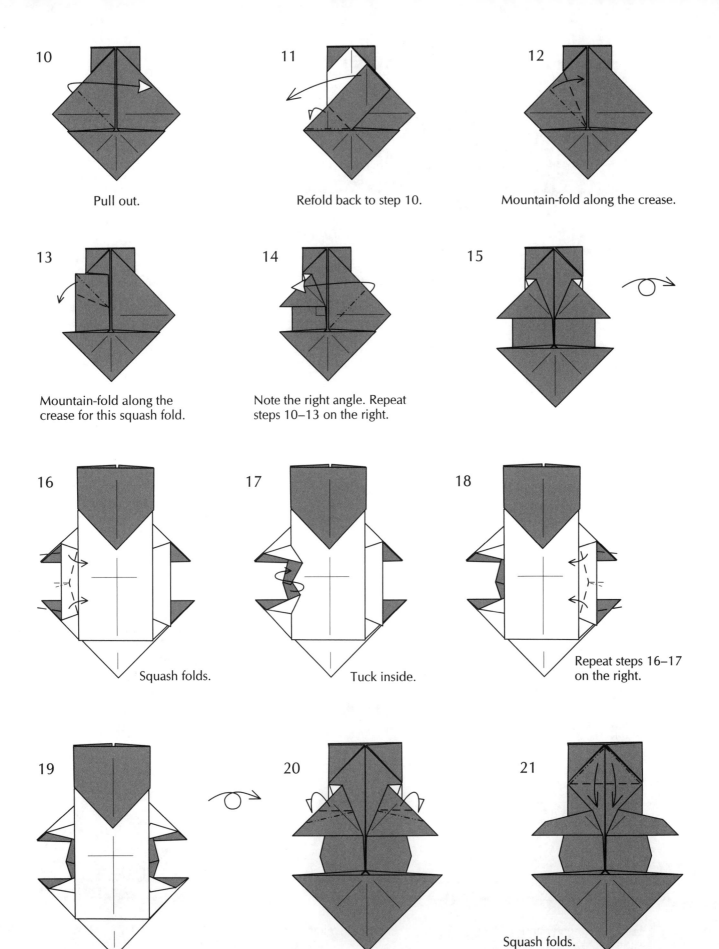

10

Pull out.

11

Refold back to step 10.

12

Mountain-fold along the crease.

13

Mountain-fold along the crease for this squash fold.

14

Note the right angle. Repeat steps 10–13 on the right.

15

16

Squash folds.

17

Tuck inside.

18

Repeat steps 16–17 on the right.

19

20

21

Squash folds.

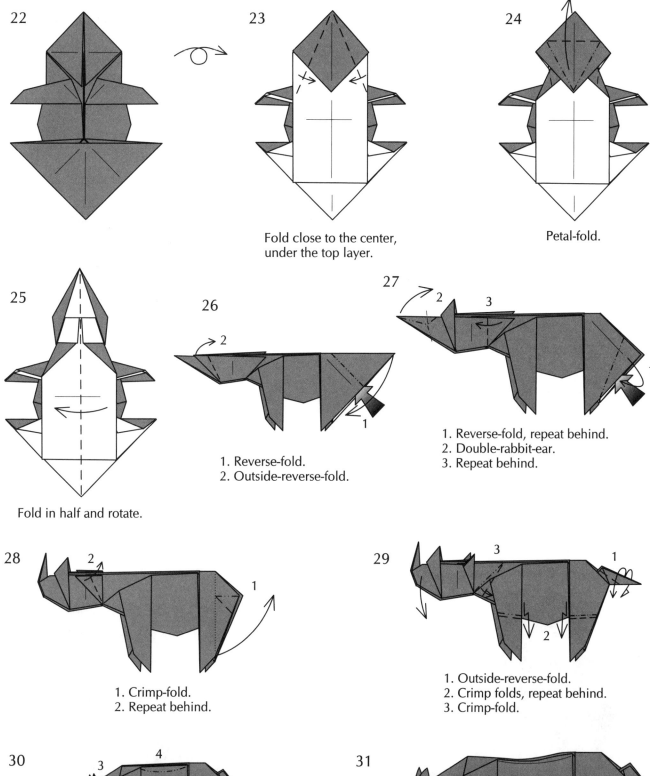

22

23

Fold close to the center,
under the top layer.

24

Petal-fold.

25

Fold in half and rotate.

26

1. Reverse-fold.
2. Outside-reverse-fold.

27

1. Reverse-fold, repeat behind.
2. Double-rabbit-ear.
3. Repeat behind.

28

1. Crimp-fold.
2. Repeat behind.

29

1. Outside-reverse-fold.
2. Crimp folds, repeat behind.
3. Crimp-fold.

30

Shape the feet, head, open the ears,
and shape the back. Repeat behind.

31

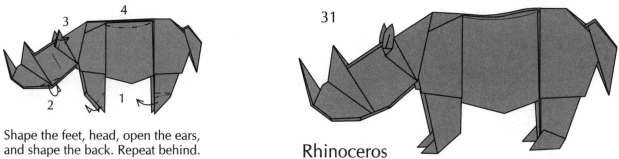

Rhinoceros

Dog Base

The Dog Base is another example of Structure & Proportion. Its proportions can easily be changed to form a variety of animals.

The Dog Base can be folded from steps 1–27 of the horse and the remaining steps here:

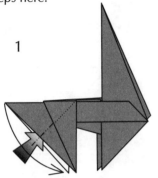

1

Begin with step 27 of the horse. Reverse-fold the tail down.

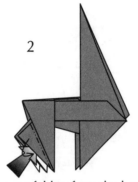

2

Reverse-fold to form the back legs and tail. Repeat behind.

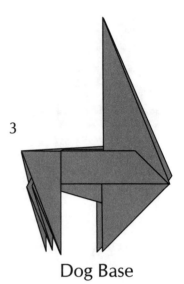

3

Dog Base

The first three steps of the Dog Base are shown here. By changing the fold in step 3 and continuing with the rest of the folds, the same structure can be formed with a range of proportions to suit a variety of animals.

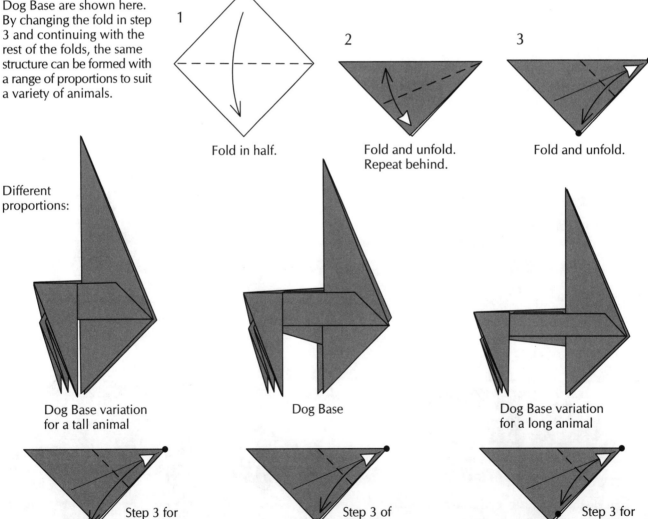

1

Fold in half.

2

Fold and unfold. Repeat behind.

3

Fold and unfold.

Different proportions:

Dog Base variation for a tall animal

Dog Base

Dog Base variation for a long animal

Step 3 for tall animal.

Step 3 of Dog Base.

Step 3 for long animal.

Horse

The horse begins with the Dog Base. As the name implies, many dogs can be formed from this base. Would you like to create some dogs or other animals from it or its variations to make taller or longer?

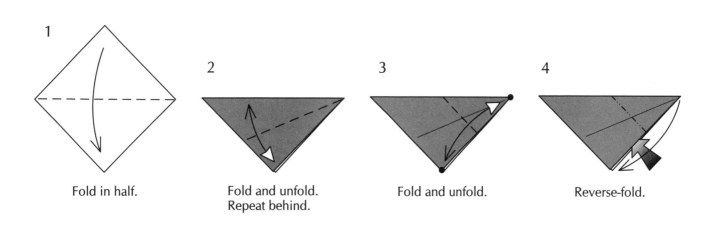

1

Fold in half.

2

Fold and unfold.
Repeat behind.

3

Fold and unfold.

4

Reverse-fold.

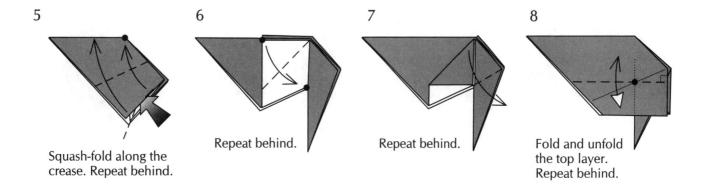

5

Squash-fold along the crease. Repeat behind.

6

Repeat behind.

7

Repeat behind.

8

Fold and unfold the top layer. Repeat behind.

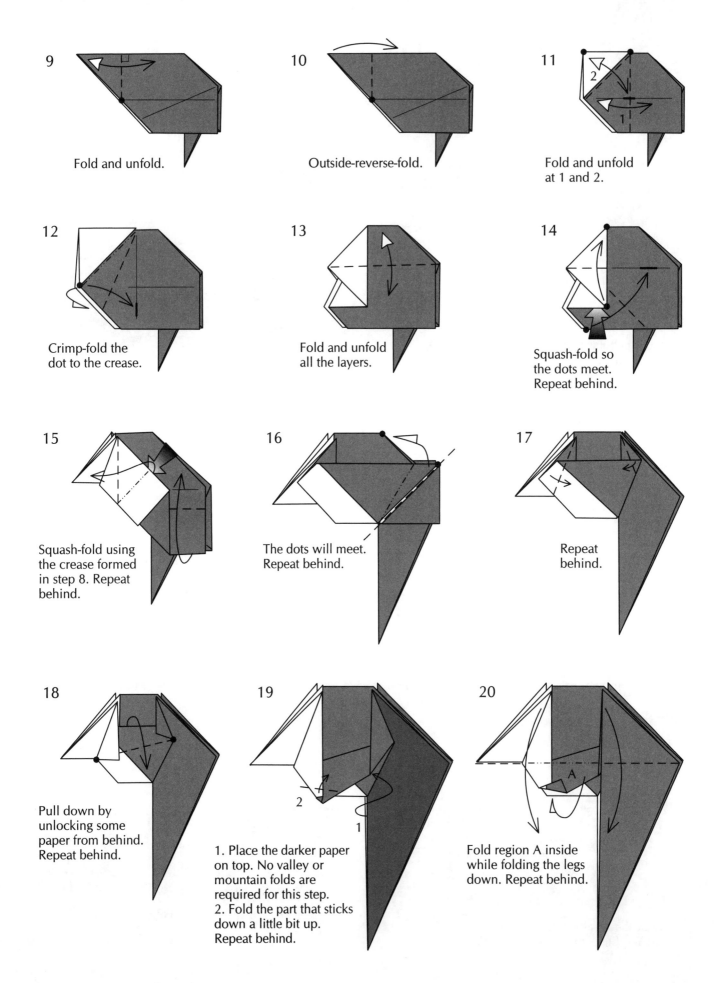

9 Fold and unfold.

10 Outside-reverse-fold.

11 Fold and unfold
at 1 and 2.

12 Crimp-fold the
dot to the crease.

13 Fold and unfold
all the layers.

14 Squash-fold so
the dots meet.
Repeat behind.

15 Squash-fold using
the crease formed
in step 8. Repeat
behind.

16 The dots will meet.
Repeat behind.

17 Repeat
behind.

18 Pull down by
unlocking some
paper from behind.
Repeat behind.

19 1. Place the darker paper
on top. No valley or
mountain folds are
required for this step.
2. Fold the part that sticks
down a little bit up.
Repeat behind.

20 Fold region A inside
while folding the legs
down. Repeat behind.

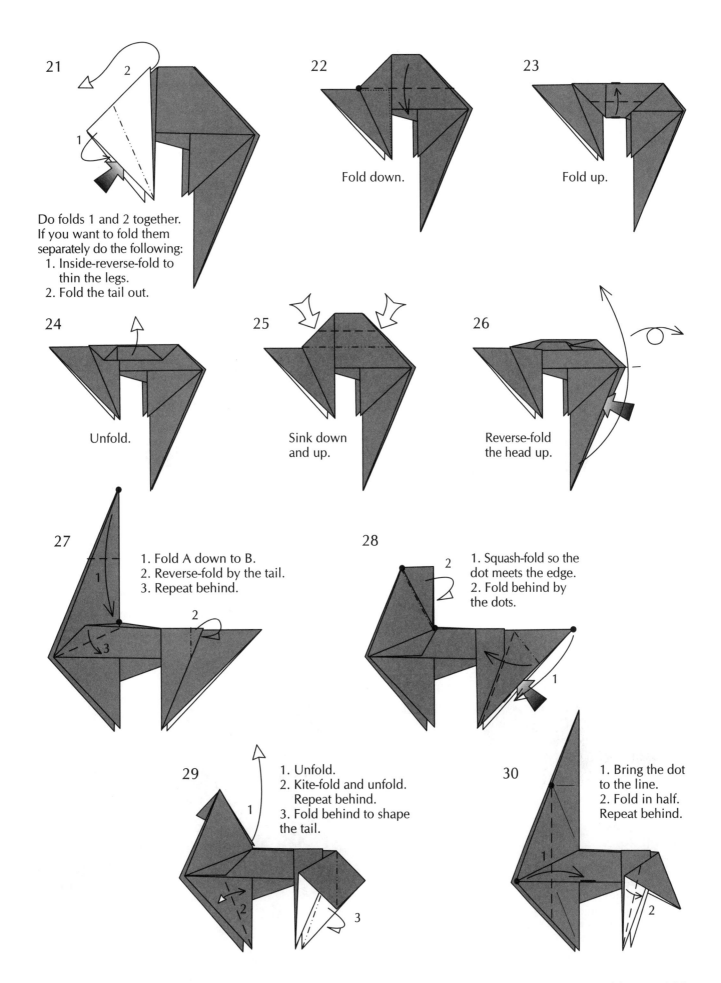

21

Do folds 1 and 2 together.
If you want to fold them
separately do the following:
1. Inside-reverse-fold to
   thin the legs.
2. Fold the tail out.

22

Fold down.

23

Fold up.

24

Unfold.

25

Sink down
and up.

26

Reverse-fold
the head up.

27

1. Fold A down to B.
2. Reverse-fold by the tail.
3. Repeat behind.

28

1. Squash-fold so the
   dot meets the edge.
2. Fold behind by
   the dots.

29

1. Unfold.
2. Kite-fold and unfold.
   Repeat behind.
3. Fold behind to shape
   the tail.

30

1. Bring the dot
   to the line.
2. Fold in half.
   Repeat behind.

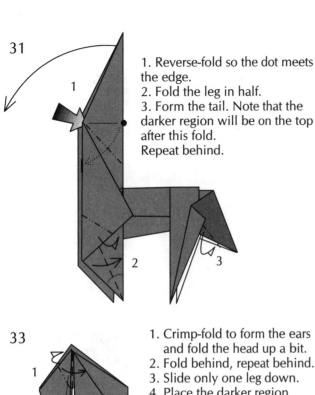

31

1. Reverse-fold so the dot meets the edge.
2. Fold the leg in half.
3. Form the tail. Note that the darker region will be on the top after this fold.
Repeat behind.

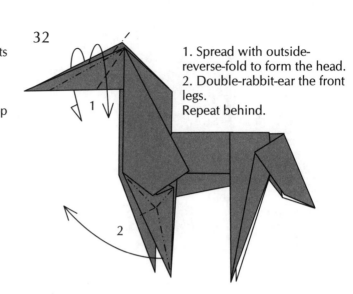

32

1. Spread with outside-reverse-fold to form the head.
2. Double-rabbit-ear the front legs.
Repeat behind.

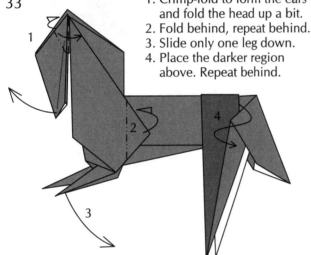

33

1. Crimp-fold to form the ears and fold the head up a bit.
2. Fold behind, repeat behind.
3. Slide only one leg down.
4. Place the darker region above. Repeat behind.

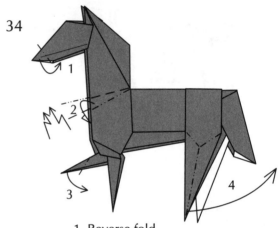

34

1. Reverse-fold.
2. Crimp-fold to bend the neck.
3. Reverse-fold the front leg.
4. Double-rabbit-ear the hind leg. Repeat behind.

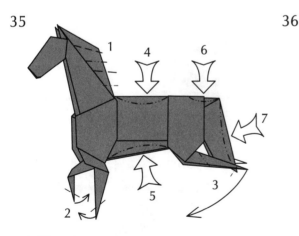

35

1. Pleat the mane.
2. Form the front hooves.
3. Shape the hind legs and hooves.
4. Make the back 3D.
5. Make the underside 3D.
6. Shape the top of the tail.
7. Shape the tail.

36

Horse

Simple Elephant

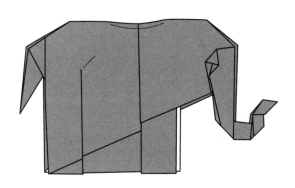

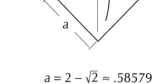

$$a = 2 - \sqrt{2} \approx .58579$$

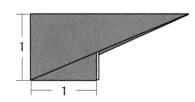

Here is a trio of elephants, simple, intermediate, and complex. They have similar proportions but different structures to allow varying detail. The simple elephant has the same structure as the intermediate elephant, dromedary, and camel. The landmark to set up the proportions yields a base where the width and height are the same. The folds for the legs in step 10 change those proportions so the elephant is taller than wide.

1

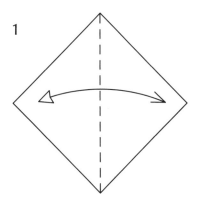

Fold and unfold.

2

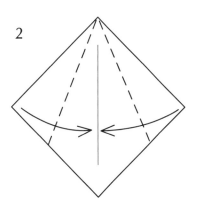

Kite-fold.

3

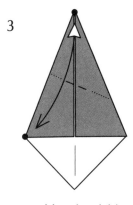

Fold and unfold in the center.

4

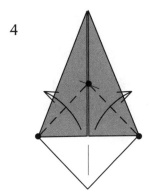

5

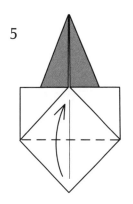

6

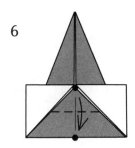

7

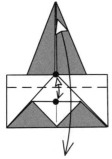

Fold and unfold.

8

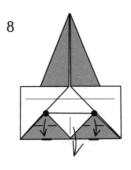

Slide the corner down so the dots meet the edge.

9

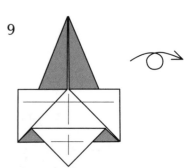

10

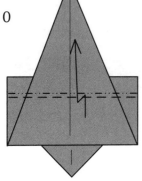

Mountain-fold along the crease for this thin pleat fold.

11

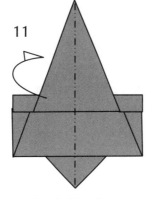

Fold in half and rotate.

12

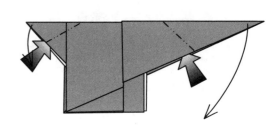

Reverse folds.

13

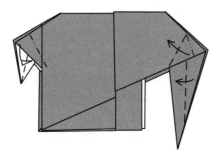

Repeat behind.

14

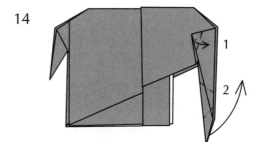

1. Squash-fold, repeat behind.
2. Reverse folds.

15

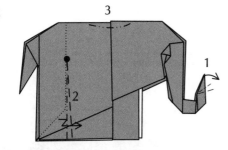

1. Spread the tip of the trunk.
2. Pleat-fold against hidden layers.
Puff out at the dot and repeat behind.
3. Shape the back.

16

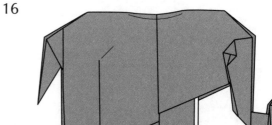

Simple Elephant

Intermediate Elephant

This elephant uses a similar structure as the simple elephant but different proportions to make the legs.

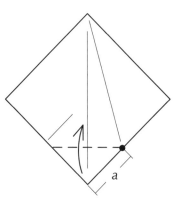

$a = 1 - \tan(30°) \approx .4226$

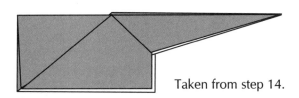

Taken from step 14.

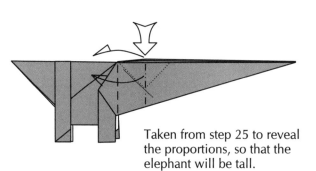

Taken from step 25 to reveal the proportions, so that the elephant will be tall.

1

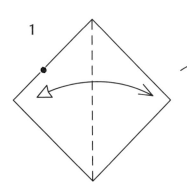

Fold and unfold.

2

 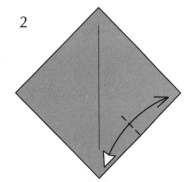

Fold and unfold at the edge.

3

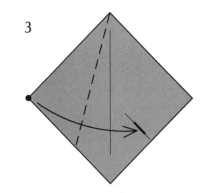

Fold the corner to the line.

4

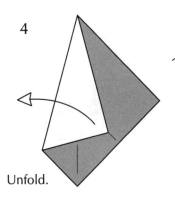

Unfold.

5

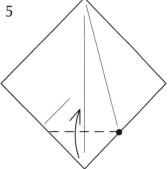

6

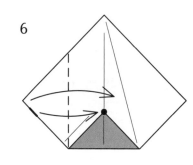

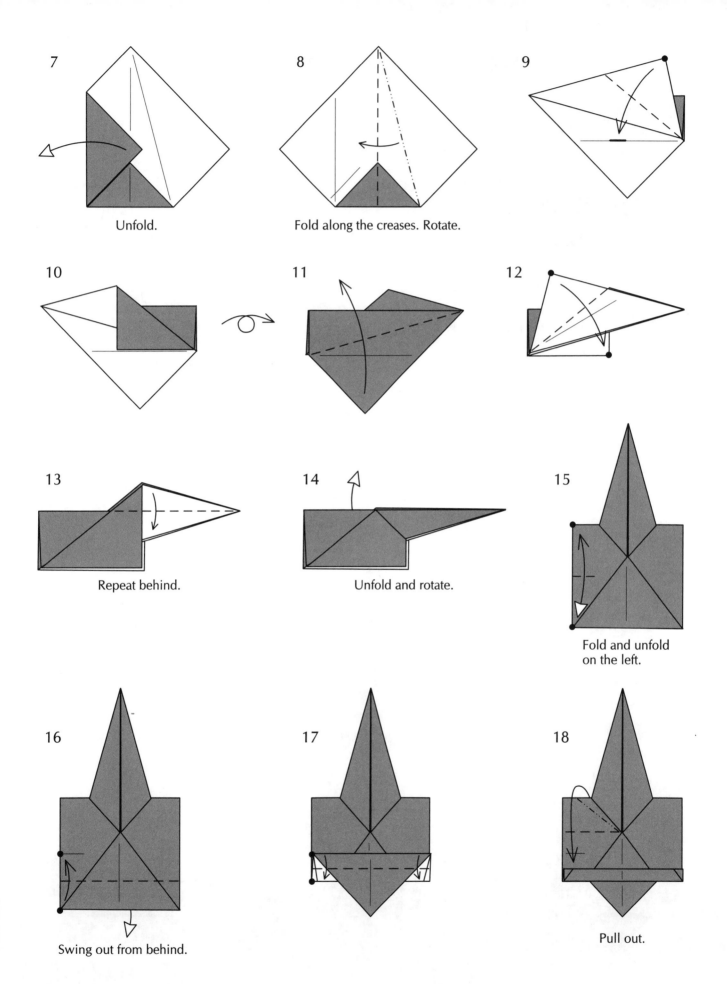

7

Unfold.

8

Fold along the creases. Rotate.

9

10

11

12

13

Repeat behind.

14

Unfold and rotate.

15

Fold and unfold
on the left.

16

Swing out from behind.

17

18

Pull out.

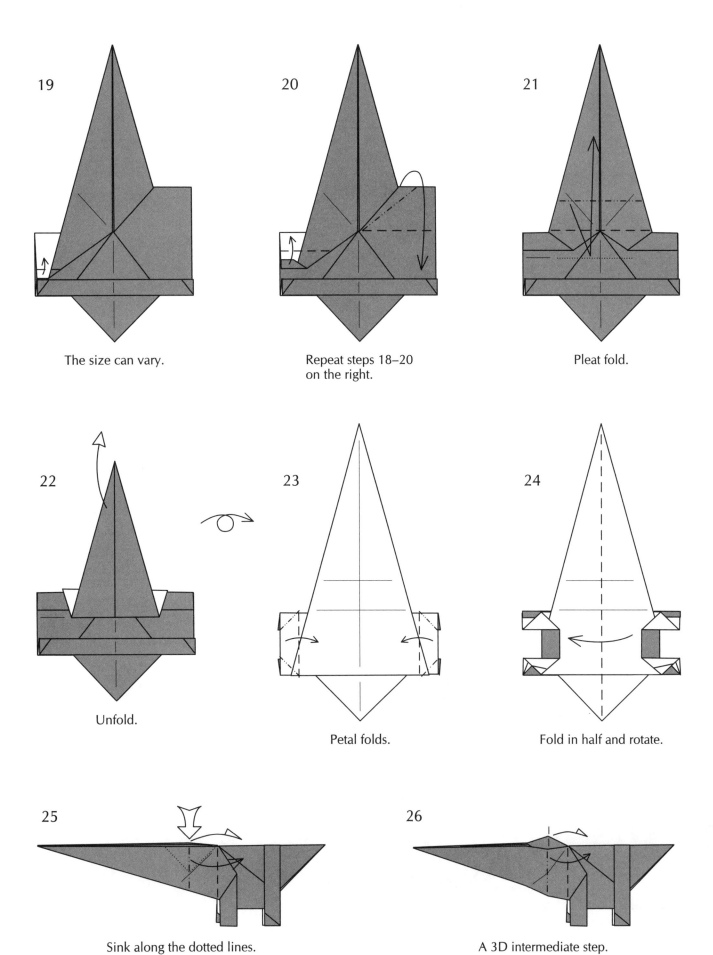

19

The size can vary.

20

Repeat steps 18–20
on the right.

21

Pleat fold.

22

Unfold.

23

Petal folds.

24

Fold in half and rotate.

25

Sink along the dotted lines.

26

A 3D intermediate step.

27

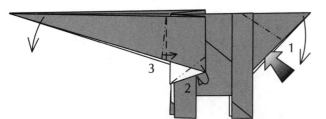

1. Reverse-fold.
2. Repeat behind.
3. Crimp-fold.

28

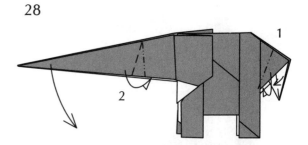

1. Thin the tail and repeat behind.
2. Crimp-fold.

29

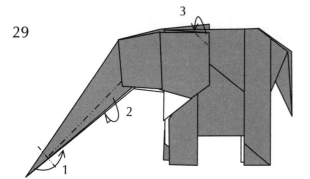

1. Reverse-fold.
2. Thin the trunk.
3. Reverse-fold.
Repeat behind.

30

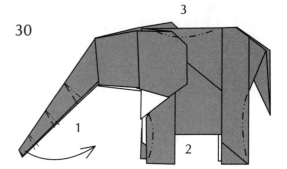

1. Shape the trunk with crimp folds.
2. Curve and shape the legs.
3. Shape the back.

31

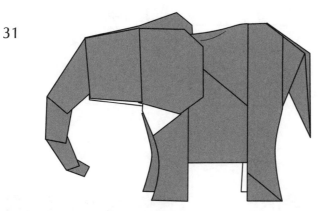

Intermediate Elephant

Complex Elephant

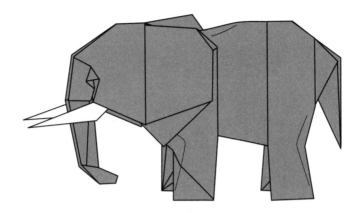

This elephant has the same proportions as the other ones, but with more detail, such as big ears and white tusks. The tusks come from opposite corners. The paper is divided into thirds. The structure allows this elephant to be folded efficiently in under 50 steps.

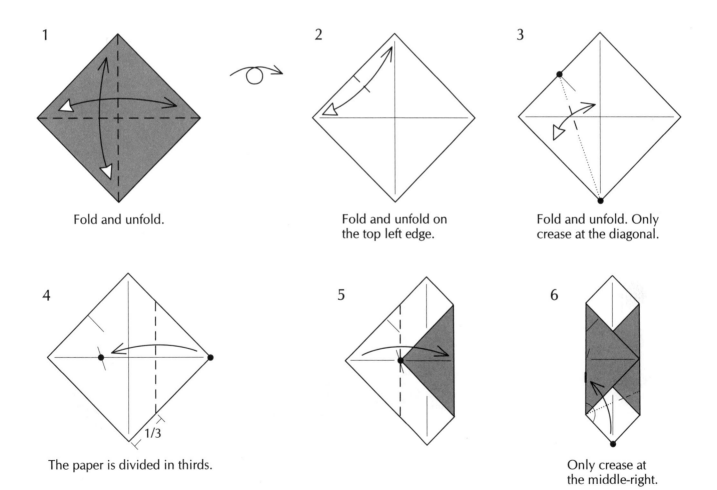

1

Fold and unfold.

2

Fold and unfold on the top left edge.

3

Fold and unfold. Only crease at the diagonal.

4

1/3

The paper is divided in thirds.

5

6

Only crease at the middle-right.

7

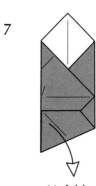

Unfold.

8

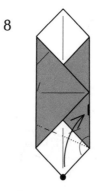

Repeat steps 6–7
on the right.

9

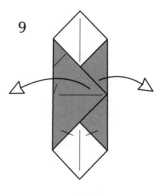

Unfold.

10

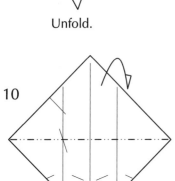

11

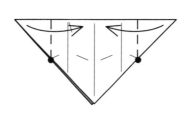

12

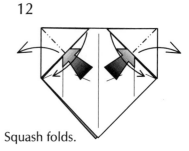

Squash folds.

13

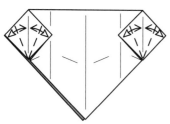

Kite-fold and unfold
on both sides.

14

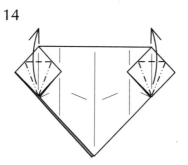

Petal folds.

15

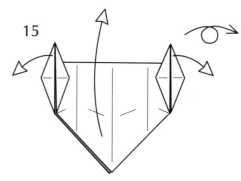

Unfold everything.

16

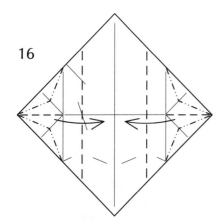

Fold along the creases.

17

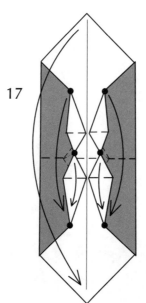

The model is 3D.
Fold in half to
flatten. The dots
will meet.

18

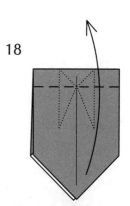

Fold the top layer up.

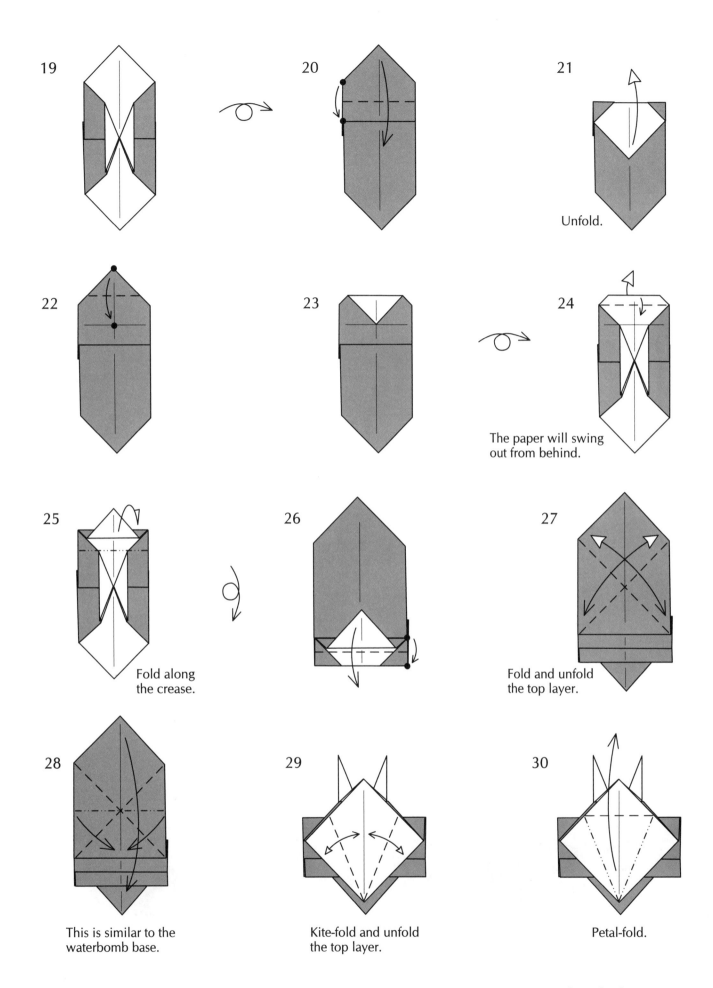

19

20

21

Unfold.

22

23

24

The paper will swing
out from behind.

25

Fold along
the crease.

26

27

Fold and unfold
the top layer.

28

This is similar to the
waterbomb base.

29

Kite-fold and unfold
the top layer.

30

Petal-fold.

Complex Elephant 113

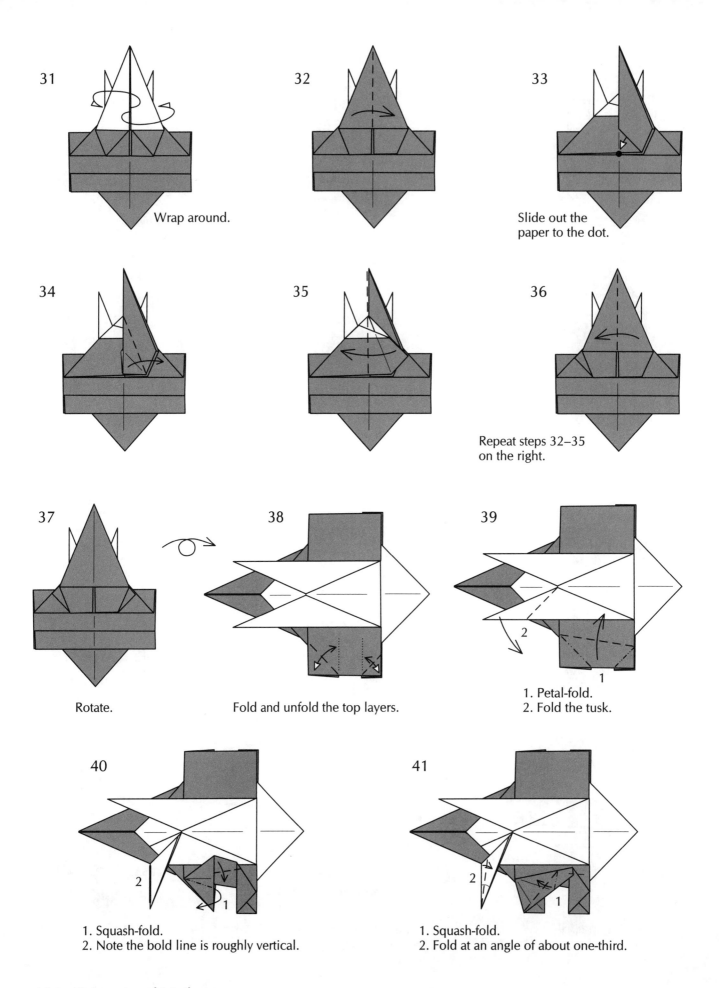

31

Wrap around.

32

33

Slide out the
paper to the dot.

34

35

36

Repeat steps 32–35
on the right.

37

Rotate.

38

Fold and unfold the top layers.

39

1. Petal-fold.
2. Fold the tusk.

40

1. Squash-fold.
2. Note the bold line is roughly vertical.

41

1. Squash-fold.
2. Fold at an angle of about one-third.

42

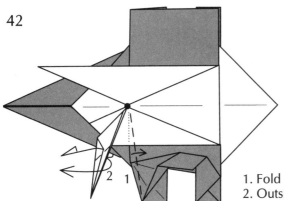

1. Fold a thin strip.
2. Outside-reverse-fold.

43

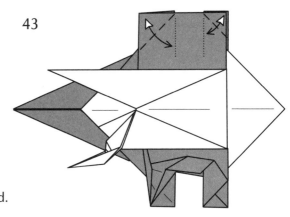

Repeat steps 38–42.

44

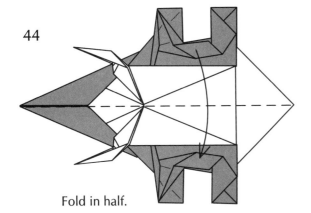

Fold in half.

45

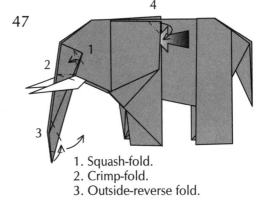

Reverse folds.

46

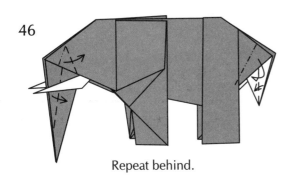

Repeat behind.

47

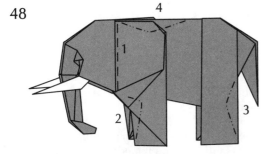

1. Squash-fold.
2. Crimp-fold.
3. Outside-reverse fold.
4. Reverse-fold.
Repeat behind.

48

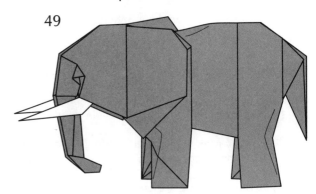

1. Shape the ears.
2 and 3. Shape the legs.
4. Shape the back.
Repeat behind.

49

Complex Elephant

On the Edge

Many models use a key landmark on the edge that sets up the rest of the folds. Math is used to calculate the landmark. The big question is, how do you fold to that landmark? You hope to use just a few simple folds but to find such a method would take huge amounts of calculations. So I have written a computer program, On the Edge, to run through thousands or millions of possibilities, and output the best solutions.

This procedure was used for several models in this book. This includes the Pentagon, Five-Sided Square, and others.

Suppose I am given a point, a, on the right edge. By doing a simple fold, new points on the edge are found. Several possible simple folds can be done using a, making a list of several new points found on the edges. If more folds are done to each of the new points, a huge number of possible landmarks can be generated.

Given a, landmark $1 - a$ is also found without doing any folds, except for turning the paper over. Thus, for every landmark a, $1 - a$ is also considered and thus added to the list of possibilities.

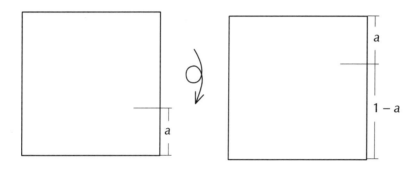

Given point a on the right edge, three points b, c, and d can be found by dividing in fourths:

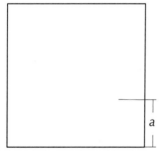

Landmark a is given.

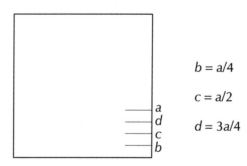

$b = a/4$

$c = a/2$

$d = 3a/4$

Landmarks b, c, and d can be calculated.

Three more landmarks, e, f, and g have also been found, each being $1 - \{b, c, \text{ or } d\}$.

With this method alone, given a starting landmark, six new ones can be found. Applying the same to each would give $6 \times 6 = 36$ landmarks. Applied again would be $6^3 = 216$ generated landmarks.

There are many more types of simple folds to consider. Suppose there are enough simple folds to generate 28 new landmarks. Then, with only four folds from an initial landmark, $28^4 = 614656$ landmarks on the edge can be found!

A simple computer program could find the method to fold to a landmark. Now I will show some of the simple folds that can be applied to a landmark on the right. Any of the landmarks found can be used again by orienting the square so the new landmark is always on the right edge, with a new series of landmarks to be generated.

Simple folds to generate more landmarks, given one on the right edge.

1. Divisions of 1/4

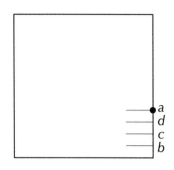

$b = .25a$

$c = .5a$

$d = .75a$

2. To a Point

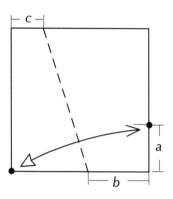

$$b = \frac{1-a^2}{2}$$

$$c = \frac{\left(1-a\right)^2}{2}$$

3. To the Edge

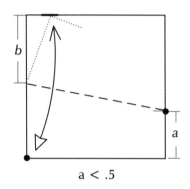

$a < .5$

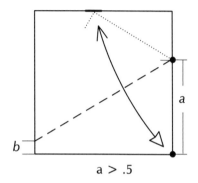

$a > .5$

$$b = \begin{cases} \sqrt{2a} - a & \text{for } a < .5 \\ a - \sqrt{2a-1} & \text{for } a > .5 \end{cases}$$

4. To a Line

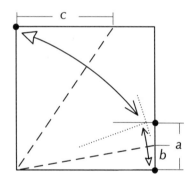

$$b = \frac{1 - \sqrt{1-a^2}}{a}$$

$$c = \frac{\sqrt{1-a^2}}{1+a}$$

5. Bisect

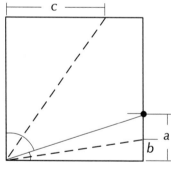

$$b = \frac{\sqrt{a^2+1}-1}{a}$$

$$c = \sqrt{a^2+1} - a$$

6. Bisect(2)

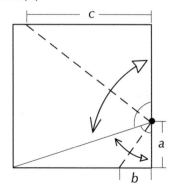

$$b = a\left(\sqrt{a^2+1} - a\right)$$

$$c = (1-a)\left(\sqrt{a^2+1} + a\right)$$

7. Point & Edge

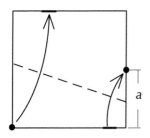

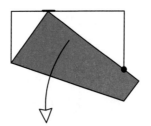

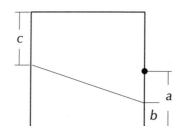

$$b = \frac{2a^2}{(1+a)^2}$$

$$c = \frac{2a}{(1+a)^2}$$

Bring the lower left corner to the top edge and the bottom edge to the landmark on the right.

Unfold.

8. Diagonal

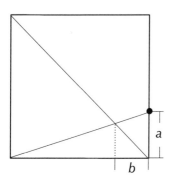

$$b = \frac{1}{a+1}$$

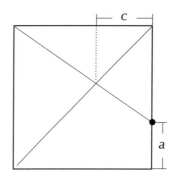

$$c = \frac{1}{2-a}$$

On the Edge Routine

We now have a collection of several simple folds that generate new landmarks from one given landmark. These are not all the possible such folds, but they give a good selection. Each of these methods shows how to generate 1, 2, or 3 new landmarks. Actually, the number is double, for if b is a new landmark, so is $1 - b$. Thus, with eight types of simple folds, 32 new landmarks are generated. A combination of two folds gives $32^2 = 1024$ landmarks. Four folds from the initial landmark yield $32^4 = 1,048,576$ possibilities. (Indeed, some are repeats, but it is still a lot!)

A computer program can go as follows:

1. Ask for landmark x.
2. Start with $a = .5$. (Fold the paper in half on the right edge.)
3. First loop: Find the 32 landmarks generated and label each as b. For each b, find the error where
    error = abs($b - x$).
If the error is small enough (you can choose it to be .001, .0001, or whatever you want) then print out which fold was done, the value of b, and the error. Then continue with the program to find more suitable folding sequences.
4. Second loop: Find the 32 new landmarks for each b and label as c. For each c, find the error where
    error = abs($c - x$).
If the error is small enough, print out the values of b and c, which folds were done, and the error. Again, continue with the program.
5. Third loop: Find all new landmarks from c and label as d. Repeat with the error and print message.
6. Fourth loop: Find all new landmarks from d and label as e. Repeat with the error and print message.

Basic Folds

Rabbit Ear.

To fold a rabbit ear, one corner is
folded in half and laid down to a side.

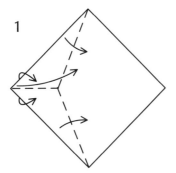

Fold a rabbit ear.

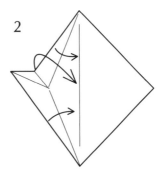

A 3D intermediate step.

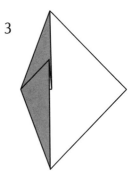

Squash Fold.

In a squash fold, some paper is opened
and then made flat. The shaded arrow
shows where to place your finger.

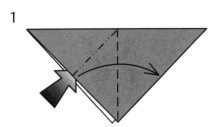

Squash-fold.

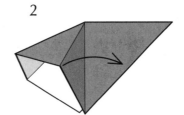

A 3D intermediate step.

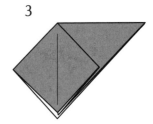

Petal Fold.

In a petal fold, one point is folded up while
two opposite sides meet each other.

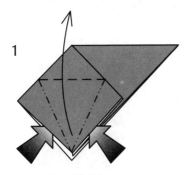

Petal-fold.

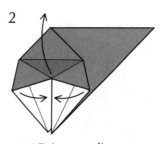

A 3D intermediate step.

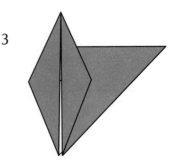

Inside Reverse Fold.

In an inside reverse fold, some paper is folded between layers. Here are two examples.

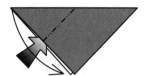

Reverse-fold.

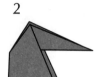

Reverse-fold.

Outside Reverse Fold.

Much of the paper must be unfolded to make an outside reverse fold.

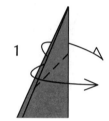

Outside-reverse-fold.

Crimp Fold.

A crimp fold is a combination of two reverse folds.

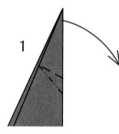

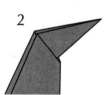

Crimp-fold.

Sink Fold.

In a sink fold, some of the paper without edges is folded inside. To do this fold, much of the model must be unfolded.

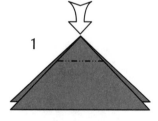

Sink.

Spread Squash Fold.

A cross between a squash fold and sink fold, some paper in the center is spread apart and then made flat.

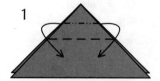

Spread-squash-fold.